The Primary School and Equal Opportunities

INTERNATIONAL PERSPECTIVES ON GENDER ISSUES

edited by Gaby Weiner

CASSELL

Cassell Educational Limited
Villiers House
41/47 Strand
London WC2N 5JE

First published 1990

British Library Cataloguing in Publication Data
The primary school and equal opportunities: international perspectives on gender issues.
1. Europe. Primary schools. Students. Girls. Education. Equality of opportunity
I. Weiner, Gaby
372.1822

ISBN: 0–304–31789–6 (hardback)
       0–304–31792–6 (paperback)

Phototypeset by Input Typesetting Ltd, London
Printed and bound in Great Britain by
Biddles Ltd, Guildford and King's Lynn

Contents

Foreword

THE EUROPE OF THE TWENTY-THREE

The Council of Europe, with a membership of twenty-three European parliamentary democracies, is the largest of the European political institutions. It represents a total population of some 400 million citizens across the breadth and depth of Europe – from Iceland to Turkey, from Portugal to Norway.

Founded in 1949, the Council of Europe was the first European political organization set up after the Second World War. It stemmed from an idea expressed by Winston Churchill in 1943 that, in addition to the proposed United Nations, regional councils would be required to deal with the problems facing the world after the war. The idea took root and was developed by the leading political figures of the post-war period.

On 5 May 1949 the Statute of the Council of Europe was signed by the ten founding states: Belgium, France, Denmark, Ireland, Italy, Luxembourg, the Netherlands, Norway, Sweden, the United Kingdom. It was unanimously agreed that, to symbolize post-war reconciliation, the headquarters of the organization should be in the French frontier city of Strasbourg, the capital of Alsace.

The aims of the Council are:

- to work for greater European unity;
- to uphold the principles of parliamentary democracy and human rights; and
- to improve living conditions and promote human values.

It also seeks to develop the common features shared by all the peoples of Europe: the 'European dimension' to their lives. Thus although the Council's work is largely carried out through intergovernmental co-operation, the interests of the individual remain its prime concern.

The Council of Europe's Statute declares that each member

state must recognize the principle of the rule of law and guarantee its citizens the enjoyment of human rights and fundemental freedoms. Any European state that accepts these democratic principles can apply to become a member. Since 1949 the membership has grown from ten to twenty-three countries, with the accession of Austria, Cyprus, Finland, the Federal Republic of Germany, Greece, Iceland, Liechtenstein, Malta, Portugal, San Marino, Spain, Switzerland and Turkey.

The Council of Europe works in close co-operation with other international organizations such as the United Nations, the European Community and the Organization for Economic Co-operation and Development. However, the organization's particular role in international co-operation results from three characteristics which distinguish it from these:

- in *structure,* the Council is more than just a purely intergovernmental body: in addition to a Committee of Ministers it has an Assembly composed of members of national parliaments and it involves local authorities and non-governmental organizations in its deliberations;
- in *scope,* the Council covers practically all aspects of European affairs, with the exception of defence;
- in *membership,* the Council includes all the European Community states, a number of 'neutral' and 'non-aligned' countries and other European democracies who share its ideals. It also opens many of its activities to non-member states, thus extending co-operation beyond the 'twenty-three'.*

It is this combination of wide membership, general competence and a flexible structure that give the Council of Europe its unique character. Indeed, as a regional organization it has served as a model for other regional groups of countries in Africa, Asia and Latin America.

---

* Twenty-seven states take part in the Council's work on education and culture – the twenty-three plus the Holy See, Hungary, Yugoslavia and Poland.

Biographical Details of the Contributors

Carole-Anne Bennett lives in Toronto, Canada. She is presently an education officer with the Ontario Ministry of Education. She has worked with city and rural school boards in Ontario as a teacher, administrator and programme consultant/co-ordinator in both elementary and secondary schools. She is a graduate of McGill University and the Ontario Institute for Studies in Education, University of Toronto.

Doris Dick graduated in Psychology from Aberdeen University in 1976, and has a postgraduate teaching certificate and diploma in education from Moray House College, Edinburgh. She is presently working as a primary school teacher in Edinburgh, and is a member of the Steering Committee of Women in Education, in Edinburgh. She has contributed articles on equality in education to the *Times Educational Supplement* (Scotland) and the *Women's Equality Group News* (London).

Lila Blount is currently a remedial teacher in a large co-educational primary school in Dublin. Previously, she spent many years in Special Education. She is a founder member of a teacher group committed to the promotion of gender equality in education (TPGEE) and also on the executive of the Committee of the Women's Studies Association of Ireland (WSAI). She is a committed activist and lobbyist on issues of gender in education, particularly when they relate to primary education and education in the home.

Rixa Borns has worked, since 1974, as a primary school teacher in Datteln, North-rhine–Westfalia. She is currently chairwoman of the primary school teacher section of the teacher union (GEW) in North-rhine–Westfalia and has participated in a number of teacher training courses on equal opportunities. She also works part-time for the regional primary school teacher council and has published a number of articles on equal opportunities.

The **Colectivo Feminista a Favor de las Niñas** was formed in 1980 by a group of women teachers working in a state school on the outskirts of Madrid. It is made up of twelve women teachers, each with a long-standing commitment to equal opportunities, and each involved in developing non-sexist educational practices.

Sigrídur Jónsdóttir was a school teacher (1961–76) and Director for Social Studies (1978–82) and currently works at the Icelandic Ministry of Education as a Director of Studies for lower primary education (6–9 years). Since 1987 she has been head of a ministerial committee concerned with promoting sex equality in Icelandic schools. She has also organized and taught on a number of in-service training courses on sex equality at Iceland's teacher-training college.

Annika Andrae Thelin is a principal administrative officer at the Swedish Board of Education, responsible for research planning, developmental work and evaluation of state education. She gained her doctorate, on schools in sparsely populated areas, in 1980, and has also worked as a teacher and researcher at the universities of Uppsala and Göteborg. During the 1980s her main research interest has focused on equal opportunities for girls and their consequences for curriculum development and educational planning.

Gaby Weiner is currently Principal Lecturer in Curriculum Studies at South Bank Polytechnic, London. She has had a number of careers including that of primary teacher, educational researcher, and course developer and author at the Open University. She has long been committed to campaigning for greater educational equality, particularly in the areas of gender and race, and has published a number of books and articles in this area.

Introduction

This volume owes its existence to a Council of Europe seminar on equal opportunities in the European primary school, held in June 1987. The reasons for the seminar were two-fold; it was one of a number of equal opportunities initiatives undertaken by the Council of Europe and it was a consequence of increased interest in equal opportunities within education across Europe in the 1980s. Why has equality of opportunity become an increasingly important educational issue for the 1980s and 1990s? Why does sex inequality persist in certain countries rather than others? How does sex inequality relate to other forms of inequality in schooling, e.g. those of class, ethnicity, disability? How can educational initiatives on gender be incorporated into existing policy frameworks and curricula? Addressing these questions provided the basis for discussion at the seminar and has helped shape the articles in this book.

I shall attempt in this introduction first to provide a brief response to the first question – the importance of equality of opportunity as an educational issue in the last decades of the twentieth century. I shall then briefly focus on the seminar and its bearing on this book.

Concern for equality has, since the period of the Enlightenment in the eighteenth century, been related to the concept of *natural justice*. Twentieth-century demands for greater equality have likewise been predicated on the assumption that discrimination on the grounds of sex, race, colour, disability or other irrelevant distinction is contrary to natural justice and is therefore morally unacceptable. In the 1950s and 1960s, for example, research evidence from the United Kingdom and Sweden showed that schooling was both sharply divisive and heavily weighted in favour of the children of middle-class parents. This resulted in moves towards establishing non-selective, co-educational secondary schooling (see Annika Thelin's chapter in this volume). In the same period, both in the United States and in Europe, an expanding economy led to more employ-

1

ment opportunities for women. This increase in women's economic power and independence resulted in the emergence of the Women's Liberation movement and a closer analysis of social, political and economic inequalities between the sexes. During this same period, the contemporary civil rights movement in the United States began to push for greater equality, this time for black women and black men. Both these movements had a world-wide impact and contributed to a deeper understanding generally of equality issues.

The 1980s has been, to some degree, a period of world recession in which emphasis has been placed on practical policy implementation and the change process, rather than the promotion of major new equality initiatives. In my view, however, sex and other forms of inequality will re-emerge with some force as an educational policy issue for the 1990s in view of the anticipated decrease in the number of school-leavers at the same time as a growth in demand for skilled labour. So it is likely, as during World War II, that there will be increased state provision for child-care to release women workers for 'industrial' duty. There will also be renewed emphasis on the role of schooling, both primary and secondary, in the creation of a non-differentiated workforce. Questions will be asked, for example, about whether and why children (and their parents and teachers) still continue to think in stereotypes and what teachers can do to discourage sexism and stereotyping? Why is it still so difficult to recruit women engineers and technologists when they are clearly capable of doing the job? How far do schools go towards challenging the stereotyped and narrowed career aspirations of girls? – and so on. It is hoped that in discussing some of these questions the contributors to this book will anticipate some of the problems of education in the 1990s and so help to ameliorate them.

On 22 June 1987, thirty teachers, education officers and teacher trainers came together in the Staatliche Akademie in Donaueschingen, Federal Republic of Germany, to attend the Council of Europe seminar on Equal Opportunities for Girls: the role of the primary school. People from fourteen different countries came to the seminar, the majority of whom were classroom teachers. Each had particular personal and professional perspectives based on their positions within the education system of their own country, and on their familiarity with equality issues. (Report of the seminar, see Council of Europe, 1987.)

One of the most important features of the seminar was the possibilities it offered seminar participants to exchange information about the range of equal opportunities projects and initiatives in different countries, and to make national comparisons. One of the most satisfying was that, despite some difficulties with the working language of the seminar, English, by the end of the week's seminar, national allegiances were hardly noticeable.

One of the most important things in the course was that there were fourteen nationalities together as one family having the same aim; the equality between the sexes, really together in one circle, not leaving anyone outside. (*Tellervo Huotari, from Finland*)

This book owes its existence to that seminar since the contributors first met each other there. It sets out first to expand on the papers presented at the seminar which illustrated particular national equal opportunities initiatives, and then, through individual case studies, to explore the state of the art in five other countries in Europe. In other words, the intention of this book is to make the original objectives of the seminar (i.e. to share experiences of, and information about, equal opportunities in education) available to a wider audience.

Interestingly, the papers that comprise the first part of the book, *Perspectives on Equal Opportunities*, take different approaches to equality issues in education. These are based, I suggest, on the specific political, social and cultural roles of education within each country. For instance, strategies have been influenced by the degree to which governments view education as instrumental to achieving greater social equality. Hence, where equality issues have received strong support from central government, e.g. in Ontario, Canada, progress has been swifter and more authoritative than where government support has been weak, e.g. in the United Kingdom.

Thus, initiatives promoting equal opportunities have taken different forms in different countries. They have focused in varying degrees on the importance of legislation and 'official' support, on the work of feminist teachers, on the value of in-service work and the production of resources, and on the importance of research.

3

Annika Andrae Thelin, in the first chapter, considers the development of equal opportunities in Sweden historically, showing that only comparatively recently (1969) has it become an issue for educationists. She argues that the ground has been laid by research on sex differences, though more recently feminists have questioned solutions which have been aimed at making girls more like boys. She points out that however fast or slow progress has been in Sweden, changes have been underpinned by central government legislation.

By contrast, the lack of central government interest in equal opportunities in the United Kingdom has meant that much of the pioneering work within education in the 1980s has been undertaken by teachers, either individually or collectively. In reporting on the work of feminist teachers, Gaby Weiner acknowledges the wide range of projects and developments undertaken by them but remains sceptical about whether teacher enthusiasm and commitment is sufficient to sustain progress on equal opportunities into the 1990s.

The Icelandic contribution, from Sigrídur Jónsdóttir, illustrates what can be achieved through in-service training and the development of materials in terms of generating awareness about the existence of sex inequalities in education. As the representative of one of the smallest countries in Europe, she also reports on the value of international co-operation – between the five Nordic countries of Denmark, Finland, Iceland, Norway and Sweden – in the pursuit of equality goals.

The final chapter in this section, by Carole-Anne Bennett, on sex equity developments in Ontario (note: Canada is a member state of the Council of Europe), focuses on the close relationship between educational policy and educational change. She shows that 'the creation of bias-free learning environments' demands a concerted effort on the part of educationists. According to Bennett, there needs to be a shared commitment: from central government in terms of legislation, in-service training and the production of classroom materials; from local school administrations, i.e. school boards, and individual schools in the implementation of local policy; and from teachers, whether collectively, through teachers' unions and federations, or individually, as part of their professional practice.

Part 2 of the book, *National Case Studies of Equal Opportunities: the European Picture*, reports on the state of the relations between the sexes in education in four countries not particularly noted for their pioneering work in terms of equal opportunities. The case studies have been written by teachers, and each provides a description of how the national system of education is organized as a background to more detailed discussion of how equality issues have (or have not) been addressed.

The four chapters, concerning Spain, Scotland, Ireland and the Federal Republic of Germany, have much in common in that they reveal shared concerns among primary teachers. Most have addressed, for instance, sex bias in school texts and readers, sexist attitudes of teachers, inequitable staffing patterns, and unsatisfactory relations between girls and boys in the classroom. However, there are also differences in the perspectives of the authors. The Spanish Colectivo Feminista a Favor de las Niñas criticizes the patriarchal nature of schooling and society; Doris Dick from Scotland advocates changes in teacher training, already under way; Lila Blount focuses on the necessity of raising awareness amongst Irish primary teachers; and Rixa Borns from Germany criticizes 'the feminist suggestion of separate classes for girls as a principle' and argues for transforming coeducational pedagogical forms.

However optimistic or pessimistic the authors in this volume are about the possibilities in their countries for swifter and more sustained change, the original Donaueschingen seminar and this book will, it is hoped, have made significant contributions. They have enabled a network to be created of educationists interested in equality issues among the member states of the Council of Europe, with the consequent exchange of information and support across national boundaries. This can only be welcomed as an important, if long overdue, milestone in the erratic progress within Europe towards the goal of equality.

Gaby Weiner, London   *April 1990*

REFERENCE

WEINER G., 36th European Teachers' Seminar, 'Equal opportunities for girls: the role of the primary school': Report. Council of Europe, 1987.

PART 1

PERSPECTIVES ON EQUAL OPPORTUNITIES

CHAPTER 1

Working Towards Equal Opportunities: The Swedish Context

Annika Andrae Thelin

This chapter describes the work carried out by the Swedish National Board of Education in the field of equal opportunities, with particular emphasis on the primary school. It not only focuses on the situation today but on the historical background to that situation. It poses suggestions for future action. What do we want the future to look like? In what ways can politicians, planners, researchers, administrators and teachers help to promote change?

My purpose is to examine the ways in which the Swedish education system has addressed the issue of equal opportunities in the last twenty-five years, during the period of the great school reforms. In my view, primary teachers and parents of primary pupils need to know much more about the context in which education takes place in order to be aware of, and to understand, the development of sex-stereotyped attitudes, classroom behaviour, differences in language use, etc.

Swedish educational policy and practice in the area of equal opportunities can be understood under the following headings:

1. Women and men in Swedish society today;
2. Legislation which has addressed equal opportunities issues;
3. Curriculum, school and post-school reforms relating to equal opportunities for girls and boys in school and young women and young men after compulsory education.
4. Policy and practice. Some centrally initiated projects and some relevant research.

WOMEN AND MEN IN SWEDISH SOCIETY TODAY

Social patterns have had a major impact on schooling. During the last fifteen years the percentage of women in the labour force has increased from 65 per cent in 1970 to about 88 per cent in 1984. The corresponding percentage of men has remained almost the same during these years, that is to say 95 per cent. There have also been differences in employment patterns between age groups. Those aged between twenty-five and fifty-four years old have the highest figures for employment and those aged between sixteen and nineteen years old have the lowest. Moreover, young women are more likely to be unemployed than young men. However, at the time of writing, total unemployment in Sweden is low, about 3 per cent.

Women work part-time more often than men and part-time employment has increased most significantly for women during the last fifteen years. Occupational patterns for men have remained much the same during these years, i.e. almost all in full-time work (Figure 1, *see p. 28*). Average income is lower for women than for men with full-time employment, but this differential does not apply to part-time workers (Figure 2, *see p. 29*).

Women and men appear very 'traditional' in their choice of employment in the industrial sector. Most women are located in the public and service sectors, while building and construction is heavily male-dominated. Moreover, women are employed in fewer sectors than men. In 1980, the structures of the twenty most popular occupations indicated that the labour force is organized on traditional, deeply sex-stereotyped lines (Figure 3, *see p. 30*). Half of those gainfully employed in 1980 worked in the twenty most popular occupations: 60 per cent of all women and 40 per cent of all men. The nine most popular occupations among women and the ten most popular occupations among men are included in these.

This pattern is also reflected in the secondary school. In 1982/3, upper secondary school leavers were strongly stereotyped in their choice of courses, reflecting either exclusively female or exclusively male worlds (Figure 4, *see pp. 31–2*). None the less, today about 95 per cent of all young men and women complete their upper secondary education in Sweden.

Interestingly, women and men use their time differently. A 1982/3 survey on the amount of time spent on work, studies,

Table 1 Who looks after whom?

Care of 0- to 6-year-olds in 1983[1]

Type of care	Percentage of all children	Percentage of all children with parents gainfully employed/ studying for at least 16 hours/week
Parents/custodian at home	44	24
Private, paid care	10	13
Other method	5	6
Part-time group only[2]	3	2
Municipal care centres	38	55

Care of 7- to 10-year-olds in 1982[3]

Type of care	Percentage of all children	Percentage of all children with parents gainfully employed/ studying for at least 16 hours/week
Parents/custodian at home	49	33
Unattended	15	19
Private, paid care	7	8
Other method	8	10
Municipal care centres	22	30

[1] Virtually all children below 1 year are at home.
[2] All 6-year-olds and in some cases 5-year-olds are entitled to part-time kindergarten amounting to about 15 hrs/week.
[3] Social service legislation sets 12 years as the cut-off limit for municipal care centres. This survey includes 7- to 10-year-olds only.

Source: *Child care survey*, November 1982–March 1983. SMS 1983:11.12.

housework and repairs showed that, in all age groups, the total time spent in paid employment, studies and housework is greater for women than for men. Women in all age groups also spent more time on housework (Figure 5, *see p. 33*). This pattern held for different age groups, but there were significant differences between women of different ages (Figure 6, *see p. 34*). Marriage and child-care seem to change the lives of young women dramatically, and women appeared to assume responsibility for housework at the expense of their own paid work and leisure time.

The organization of child-care is important in this context. Almost 50 per cent of all children aged up to ten years are taken care of by their parents or guardians at home. Thirty-eight per cent of the younger ones (up to six years old) are looked after at municipal care centres. These figures are higher for younger children and where parents (mothers) are in paid employment, as working mothers are more likely to be able to pay for child-care where municipal provision is low (Table 1).

What messages does this daily experience of stereotyping in the home give to young children? Do they play an active part in household work themselves, and if so in what way? The survey mentioned earlier includes some questions on housework done by children. Girls and boys in the younger age group do roughly equal amounts and kinds of work. However, older girls are more likely than older boys to perform 'women's' tasks such as cooking, washing up and cleaning. Boys are more likely to do gardening and run errands (Tables 2 and 3).

Table 2 Work performed by children in the home 1982–1983 (percentage breakdown by age group).

Hours/week	Girls		Boys	
	5–10 years	11–18 years	5–10 years	11–18 years
	%	%	%	%
0	47	25	51	43
1	13	9	22	16
2	22	23	11	15
3	7	17	7	13
4–7	9	14	6	8
8+	2	12	4	5
Total	100	100	100	100
Average hours/week	1.5	2.9	1.3	1.7

Girls and boys in the younger age group do roughly the same amount and type of work. In the older age group, girls are more inclined than boys to perform traditional women's chores such as cooking, washing up and cleaning. Boys are more likely to do gardening and run errands.

In public life, women represent half the population in Sweden yet turn out in proportionally larger numbers at national elections. None the less the influence exerted by women in

Table 3 Participation of children in different types of housework 1982–1983 (percentage of girls and boys in different age groups).

Type of work	Girls		Boys	
	5–10 years	11–18 years	5–10 years	11–18 years
	%	%	%	%
Cleaning	52	65	47	48
Laying and clearing table	42	22	47	21
Washing up	17	38	17	20
Cooking	21	33	14	18
Running errands	17	22	25	29
Making beds	30	37	23	36
Washing	2	16	2	5
Babysitting brothers and sisters	9	10	9	8
Gardening	–	5	6	13

These figures do not indicate the time spent on individual types of work.
Source: National Board for Consumer Policies

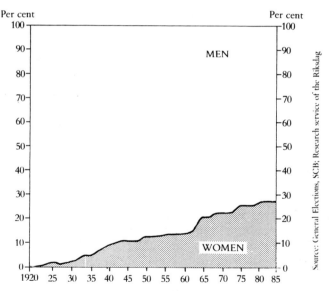

Figure 7 Membership of the Swedish Parliament (Riksdag) 1920–84 (percentage of women and men).

13

Table 4 Membership of the Swedish Parliament (Riksdag) 1985.

Party		Number		Percentage	
		Women	Men	Women	Men
M	(Conservatives)	21	65	24	76
C	(Centre Agrarian)	19	37	34	66
Fp	(Liberals)	4	17	19	81
S	(Social Democrats)	53	113	32	68
Vpk	(Communists)	4	16	20	80
All parties		101	248	29	71

Source: Research Service of the Riksdag.

Table 5 Elected members of county councils and elected members of county council regional boards after 1982 election.

Party		Number		Percentage	
		Women	Men	Women	Men
M	(Conservatives)	111	252	31	69
C	(Centre Agrarian)	100	204	33	67
Fp	(Liberals)	25	77	25	75
S	(Social Democrats)	293	556	35	65
Vpk	(Communists)	28	50	36	64
KDS	(Democratic Christian Alliance)	5	16	24	76
Total		562	1155	33	67

Source: County Council's statistical year-book 1983.

legislative bodies at different levels is still very small (Figure 7). Women have gradually increased their influence, particularly over the last two decades (Tables 4, 5 and 6). Major break-throughs have taken place at middle levels in politics and the trade unions. Still, very few women hold senior executive positions in industry and the public sector.

Similar social patterns are evident in the schools. Teachers are key persons in the lives of pupils — both in their role as educators and transmitters of knowledge and attitudes and as adult professionals and human beings. Statistics on school staffing patterns speak for themselves: 99 per cent of primary

14

teachers are women; overall only 11 per cent of headteachers are women. School hierarchies follow a familiar pattern:

- The younger the children, the higher the proportion of female teachers.
- The lower the salary, the higher the proportion of female teachers.
- The lower the salary, the more working hours in school.

Moreover, Swedish teacher education has paid little attention to eliminating sex stereotyping or promoting equal opportunities.

Table 6 Elected members of municipal councils and local government committees by party on 1 January 1983.

Political party		Number		Percentage	
		Women	Men	Women	Men
M	(Conservatives)	2 597	6 357	29	71
C	(Centre Agrarian)	2 280	6 840	25	75
Fp	(Liberals)	680	1 934	26	74
S	(Social Democrats)	6 320	16 253	28	72
Vpk	(Communists)	380	772	33	67
KDS	(Democratic Christian Alliance)	138	629	18	82
MP	(Environmentalists)	79	123	39	61
Others		105	352	23	77
Independent		12	67	15	85
Total		12 591	33 327	27	73

Source: The Swedish Association of Local Authorities. Elected members of Local Government authorities 1983, by party and sex.

LAWS WHICH HAVE ADDRESSED EQUALITY ISSUES

Today all Swedish political parties officially support the idea of equal opportunities for women and men. In essence, equal opportunities has come to mean equal rights, responsibilities and opportunities for women and men alike in such areas as:

- having a job that encourages financial independence,

- caring for children and the home,
- participating in political and social life.

In 1980 Parliament passed an act prohibiting sex discrimination in the labour market (SFS, 1979:1118). Before this legislation, progress had been very slow. The following landmarks in Swedish history provide a useful background to the current debate:

1859 Women able to enter a limited number of lower-grade teaching jobs.

1873 Women entitled to take academic degrees, with a few exceptions (law and theology).

1921 Married women achieve political rights from the age of twenty-one (unmarried women had acquired them in 1874).

1927 Girls admitted to state grammar schools.

1935 Equality for women and men achieved under the national pensions scheme.

1937 Maternity benefits are introduced.

1950 Both parents become legal custodians of their children (if born in wedlock).

1969 Equal opportunities for girls and boys are stressed in the curriculum of the compulsory comprehensive school.

1974 Parental insurance is instituted, entitling both mother and father to paid leave of absence after the birth of a child.

1975 New abortion legislation allows women freedom of choice up to and including the eighteenth week of pregnancy.

1980 Parliament passes an act prohibiting sex discrimination in the labour market.

1982 Child care at home is regarded as a qualification for the national pension scheme.

1982 A ban is imposed on the display of pornographic material in public places.

1983 All occupational categories are opened to women, including the armed forces.

Looking back, it is clear that the first steps to guarantee women the same rights as men were taken in the area of employment. In recent decades, the provision of child care for women was seen as a priority, and lately attempts have been made to persuade parents to share responsibility for the home and for children. Much remains to be done, however. Laws are merely indicators of the need for change. For instance, a quota system for women and men in some occupational areas has been discussed but not yet acted upon. It is thus clear that the promotion of equal opportunities has wider social implications and needs to take place in the school, in the family, and in society at large.

What can we expect from education? How can schools address equal opportunities issues?

CURRICULUM, SCHOOL AND POST-SCHOOL REFORMS RELATING TO EQUAL OPPORTUNITIES FOR GIRLS AND BOYS IN SCHOOL AND AFTER

Education has the dual role of preserving and changing society. Which is the more important is a debatable point. Swedish school reform was predicated on the assumption that education was one of the most important agencies for promoting equality and democracy. Attitudes, norms and values, it was believed, are shaped and transmitted by the educational system.

Until the reform period started in the 1950s, the education system was sharply divisive. Sex segregation was evident both in school organization and in its curriculum content. Although Sweden has provided compulsory elementary education for girls and boys since 1842, only boys could continue their education at secondary level. Girls' municipal schools were opened in the nineteenth century, but they had different objectives and curriculum content compared to boys' grammar schools. However, the curriculum became the same in 1909 and girls were allowed into the grammar schools in 1927. Shorter courses in citizenship education, linked to compulsory education, were developed in the early twentieth century. The content of these was traditionally male- or female-oriented (housework for girls and economy for boys). Even when compulsory and within the same subject area, there were different courses for girls and boys, for example, in mathematics boys were supposed to take longer courses than girls.

The state grammar school provided boys with the means of entry to a position in the public service. In contrast, the girls' municipal school taught languages, music, etc., and 'good' behaviour in the private and family sphere. The basis for this segregation was the profound belief that girls and boys should be educated to perform different roles and have different positions in society.

The bill introducing the nine-year comprehensive school (Prop 1950:70) was passed in 1950. 'One school and the same education' became the right of every Swedish child between seven and sixteen years of age. The curriculum was controlled centrally for all schools and a new curriculum was introduced in 1962. Equal rights were to become the all-pervading objectives of education according to this curriculum. Rolling reforms during the last twenty-five years have worked to eliminate all obstacles.

However, equal opportunities between the sexes were not specially emphasized in the 1962 curriculum. The term 'equal opportunities = jämställdhet' was not used. In the guidelines, however, socialization (social education) and education for family life were to be included in specific subjects (handicraft, home economics, child care, economy). These subjects were grouped along specific lines according to sex and applied to practical work within the classroom. Nothing was said, as already indicated, about equal opportunities in these or any other area of the school curriculum.

In organizational terms, however, progress was made. At middle level, for instance, for handicraft girls were taught woodwork and boys textile work on a twenty-hour experimental course. Pupils and teachers were very pleased with this arrangement and it was gradually increased to a course of one whole term. At senior level when pupils could make individualized choices, handicraft was very popular among both boys and girls. The pupils were streamed into different lines in grade nine (age 15). Many boys chose a practical line called practical technology, which among other things included 'male' activities. Home economics was introduced as a compulsory subject for girls and boys at senior level in grade seven (age 13), as an optional subject in grade eight (age 14) and as a main subject of 'the home economics line', mainly taken by girls, in grade nine. Child-care, too, was made a general subject for both boys and girls in grade nine.

In every other subject girls and boys were taught together and the same curricula applied — except in physical education, in which pupils were taught together only up to grade four (age 10).

The curriculum was again revised in 1969. The concept of equal opportunities was introduced in the guidelines and defined in relation to family life, the labour market and society as a whole. 'Through education pupils should be informed about sex roles, encouraged to debate this topic and to question current conditions.' Within the recommendations it was stated that 'stereotypes are common obstacles to a well-grounded choice of career for girls and boys. They should be eliminated'.

Issues of equal opportunities were therefore to be promoted. Family life was to become a focus in social and natural science, Swedish, religion, and in specific subjects such as handicrafts, home economics, child care and vocational guidance. In all these subjects the curriculum guidelines advocated that sex stereotyping and equal opportunities should be addressed. But these issues were also to be dealt with in other subject areas. Textiles and woodwork were made compulsory for both girls and boys at primary level. Home economics was not yet introduced at primary and middle levels but instituted as a main subject at senior levels, and child-care became a compulsory element of home economics.

In the 1980 curriculum, promoting equal opportunities was equated with education for democracy: 'Life in a democratic society must be shaped by free and independent people. Thus school should work for equal opportunities for women and men.' Different courses, it was argued, should not encourage segregation – if so, they should be revised. Vocational guidance should focus on more detailed information from the first school year. The headteacher was given special responsibility for providing information and materials and keeping track of what was happening within different subjects. Pupils were to be encouraged to take non-traditional subject options. Pupils would be informed about inequalities in work conditions and

19

in wages for women and men. Collaboration between subjects was recommended. Every school should have a plan for the school year, which should be evaluated after the end of the school year. This plan should include equal opportunities for girls and boys. The syllabuses for various subjects were revised, and home economics was introduced at primary and middle levels. Child-care acquired a permanent place in the curriculum, and girls and boys were taught physical education together.

To sum up, the 1962 curriculum questioned the sex stereotypes of former curricula and stressed equal rights, that is to say, the reduction of social, economic and geographical inequalities. However, the term 'equal opportunities' (*jämställdhet*) was not yet used, although some smaller organizational changes were introduced.

A great step forward was taken in the 1969 curriculum with the introduction of more developed objectives and guidelines, with changes of organization and revision of syllabuses and curriculum content in different subjects. An 'equal opportunities programme' was now formulated by the National Board of Education (NBE) which incorporated these changes. In the 1980 curriculum the last discriminatory organizational barriers were removed and curriculum areas were further revised and the primary level was included. Study and vocational guidance was emphasized. Much recent educational debate has moved away from emphasis on the home and family towards labour-market concerns. It has concentrated on equal opportunities for girls, in an attempt to make girls enter professions and trades dominated by men (Table 7).

POLICY AND PRACTICE. SOME CENTRALLY INITIATED PROJECTS AND RELEVANT RESEARCH

I shall now turn to the implications of development projects and research studies for educational planners. The content of 'the Equal Opportunities Programme' (Skolöverstyrelsen, 1975: Ett friare val) is important in this context. Its perspective can be summarized as follows:

Equal opportunities refer to teaching, school structure, teaching staff and school authorities as well as to society.

Table 7 Equal opportunities for girls and boys.

Content	Curriculum		
	1962	1969	1980
Quantitative			
Goals and guidelines	+	+++	+++
Organization	+	++	+++
Subjects/items	+	++	+++
Qualitative			
Main content	o (home/ family)	o (home/ family)	—
in private and public spheres		o (labour market) o (society)	o (labour market) o (society)

+ = an increased number means an increased stress or space in the curricula.
o = content areas which are stressed in the curricula.

Every girl and boy should have the opportunity to engage in non-traditional activities and work, take part in debate and criticize the existing situation. They should be given relevant orientation and knowledge. Teachers at school should acquire a knowledge of sex stereotypes in general and especially of how they affect their own subjects. They should also be encouraged to increase their consciousness of their own import-ance as an example. Through practical and theoretical work teaching should add to every pupil's competence to manage his or her own life, to take part in family and working life, to be ready and able to take part in consultation and decision-making. Opportunities to choose various subjects and courses should be constructed in such a way as to avoid traditional sex-oriented choices.

This is a summary, and the intention is to point out the very broad interpretation and objectives of the equal opportunities programme. The programme also provides practical advice on participation for pupils, teachers, parents, headteachers and people outside school. One of its most detailed parts concerns guidance and counselling. Although the equal opportunities programme as well as the 1980 curriculum make it everyone's duty to promote equal opportunities, most commitment has come from those working in school study and vocational guidance areas. An interest in vocational guidance has also been expressed jointly by the NBE and the Ministry of Labour.

Thus, in the 1980s, economic decline, technological development and a perceived need to defend and maintain Swedish subject expertise in the world, and a diminishing number of pupils in every age group at school, has led to a back-to-basics movement parallel to an equal opportunity debate.

Efforts have clearly concentrated on getting girls into non-traditional technical courses and occupations (NBE Information 86:74). In a technological society, it was argued, girls should not be ignored but encouraged to choose non-traditionally. A parliamentary grant was given to the Ministry of Labour to establish projects in different schools to help girls make technical choices and to encourage collaboration between school and trade and industry. Although interest among pupils and teachers has been high, only a few girls continue to make non-traditional choices and the drop-out rate is still high.

Teachers at primary level and in nursery school have been given in-service training so that they are able to teach technical subjects by building on the children's daily experiences.

Another strategy has been for girls to be taught in single-sex groups, to give them a chance of developing and practising technical activities and to enable them to have more attention from the teacher — research has shown that boys dominate mixed-sex settings. Special summer courses have been arranged for girls to learn computer science. Some of these central initiatives have been further developed at regional, local and school levels has been drawn up.

Most work has been done at secondary level despite general agreement that challenging sex stereotypes should begin at an early age. However, some projects have started at pre-primary level and in collaboration with other institutions. For example, the Royal Institute of Technology in Stockholm has contributed to the production of a booklet, and the Chalmers Institute of Technology in Gothenburg has produced 'a technical box'. Seminars and lectures have been organized on such topics as:

- children's thinking;
- technology in everyday life and at home;
- girls and boys: similarities and differences;
- the teacher's role.

The above examples are measures taken to eliminate educational inequalities. Swedish school research results have also been of importance as a point of departure for these aims and directions.

According to researchers in Sweden and abroad, boys are given priority in school (NBE 86:74). An observation study of pupils in the fourth and seventh grades in a number of Swedish schools showed that boys were asked questions and given tasks to complete more often than girls. The boys received more help and encouragement but they also received more reprimands than the girls. Boys were more likely to approach the teacher and ask for help than the girls. Another study showed that girls adjust more easily to school roles and that they enjoy school more than the boys. However, girls are more anxious and afraid of failing, an anxiety which increases as they grow older (Wernersson, 1977).

In a project entitled 'Language and Sex at School' carried out at a teacher-training college the researchers found that boys talk more than girls, whether or not they are classified as talkative or quiet pupils. Boys also dominate in most debates at school. They present their opinions in a clear and confident manner. Talkative girls do not assert their opinions in the same way and are more likely to be considered 'teacher's pet'. Girls consider it more important for a discussion to lead to a conclusion and for the group to carry out its task than for their opinions to gain a hearing. Boys learn from an early age to promote their own needs and interests, whereas girls are guided more by the general good (Einarsson and Hultman, T, 1984). In an English investigation it was found that teachers often select educational material which appeals to boys' interests rather than to girls' interests. A possible explanation of this is that boys are more difficult to motivate (Spender, 1982).

Another Swedish researcher (Stage C, 1985), reports that girls start with an advantage over boys due to their earlier maturity, but boys undermine this by developing behaviour which attracts the teacher's attention. Furthermore, the only early differences identified between the sexes are differences in verbal and spatial capacity — newborn girls are more sensitive to aural stimuli and boys more sensitive to visual stimuli. When it comes to school work the setting is probably much more advantageous to boys than to girls. Boys who have problems with reading and writing in the early grades are given more attention. Girls are well socialized during their early school years when education is mostly verbal. When education becomes more spatial, at secondary level, girls experience some problems. It is then perhaps too late for them to get the same kind of attention as the boys got earlier. According to Piaget, this must take place during an earlier developmental period (i.e. the cognitive transformation period). Thus, it follows that there should be some kind of spatial training for girls in the first grade as well. Even though there have been many experiments in which girls have been encouraged to learn natural science and technology (as in the projects just mentioned) in my view the optimal conditions for teaching girls natural science remain to be investigated.

So it seems that girls need to be compensated in one way or another to reach the same level as boys. Schools, reflecting society in general, use male standards or criteria for girls to aim at. Girls should, it is argued, grow up to be as similar to boys as possible. The following questions are, however, seldom put:

- Why is it so important to have more girls in technical education?
- How can/will the presence of girls change the content, methods, aims and directions of technological subjects and the technologically orientated professions?
- How do boys *and* girls look at their lives in the longer term? How do they plan? How does school organization and content meet these needs?
- What about education and equal opportunities in the wider context? Should it not include, for all children, discussion of possibilities for career (the public sphere) and home and family life (the private sphere)?

These questions are much more difficult to incorporate into educational planning but are nevertheless important. Most of our knowledge of sex stereotypes has come from statistical descriptions and analyses and from developmental studies. The figures have consistently pointed to inequalities between the sexes. Despite important programmes for change there is evidence that the differences are still there. However, interest in research on women has increased during the 1970s, and presented the beginnings of a new perspective on sex inequality.

Researchers within this perspective have focused on the life-context of women in education. In Norway some methodological development has taken place (Skrede and Tornes' 1983 *Studier i Kvinnors Livslop*). In Sweden research has been carried out on female university students. The presumption is that jobs as well as family objectives are of substantial value for women's educational options and vocational careers while men are most often guided chiefly by a career. Women generally express a greater responsibility for the care of children and the elderly, for good relationships and for ensuring an affectionate atmosphere in the home and family. Thus, the explanation for the different life patterns of men and women is to be found outside the general scope of educational planners. Studies of life patterns and contextual structures would be fruitful in order to increase our knowledge of women in education and give planners a basis for measures to be taken at an early level of the school system. An American researcher (Eccles, 1982), in a study of girls' educational options, pointed to the need for more complex models of change strategies which, among other things, emphasizes the utility of education. The possibility of combining work outside home with family life and children is of considerable importance to girls.

This theoretical development is very close to that of a Norwegian researcher (Ve, 1982), who studied the unequal allocation of power between men and women and its implications for the socialization of boys and girls. In her view, girls are educated to care for and to take responsibility for other persons. She argues that women identify with other people's interests and thus have little status within authority- or power-dominated relations. Women often consider personal problems in other ways to men. At the same time women do not necessarily want to change because they feel that it is important to care for other people, such as handicapped people, if society is to be worth living in. Hildur Ve also argues that societal conditions should be created so that men (as well as women) are socialized into a new form of sensitivity which incorporates the best part of men's technical orientation and women's personal/human orientation – this means men sharing responsibility for family and child care (private sector) with women. This may also result in a change in authority and power relationships between the sexes in the employment sphere (public sector).

Studies like these, which use girls' and women's experiences as a starting point for theoretical discussion, offer new possibilities of broadening our knowledge and our explanations, which statistical analyses alone cannot.

Levy (1972) has put it like this:

> The first phase of the renewed feminist wave of criticism, analysis and polemic seems to have peaked and the difficult application of feminist analysis to the traditional male-based social sciences barely has begun. Studies of 'sex roles socialisation' have typically accepted the *content* of sex roles as given and have attempted to clarify the variables affecting the learning *process* along sex role lines. This objectification and reification of sex roles has prevented our understanding of how sex role learning is taught and elaborated in patriarchal society. That 'appropriate' sex role learning for girls, while functional to the maintenance of male-dominated society, is detrimental to girls' psychological development has often been acknowledged. But this fact has been overlooked in the overriding concern that schools might be 'emasculating our boys'. There is not even a word in our language to represent the 'castration' or 'emasculation' of females. We need serious research into how traditional sex role stereotypes affect girls' learning and development and how schools continue to perpetuate and develop these stereotypes. Most importantly, new educational environments must be designed to eliminate restrictive sex role learning so that girls and boys can be free to explore their full human potential.

In my view, the interests, strategies and plans of girls and young women should be as important to educational planners as those of their male peers. Girls' vocational and life choices should be respected and given serious attention, rather than looked upon as something that complicates the system. Equal opportunities policies should address job, power, authority, family life and child care — the private as well as the public sectors. Schools must take responsibility for *all* these aspects.

In other words: Girls and women are entitled to be equal on their own terms and according to their own needs, and should not be limited to the agenda set by boys and men.

REFERENCES

Eccles, J. (1982) 'Math and career achievement: A psychological model for decision-making; Bringing women to science'. *The Research News.* Sept–Oct, University of Michigan.

Einarsson, J. och Hultman, T. (1984): *Godmorgon pojkar och flickor: Om språk och kön i skolan.* Malmö: Liber Förlag.

Läroplan för grundskolan 1962 (Lgr 62) Kungl Skolöverstyrelsen, Skriftserie 60. Stockholm: Kungl Skolöverstyrelsen.

Läroplan för grundskolan 1969 (Lgr 69):, Skolöverstyrelsen, Stockholm: Svenska Utbildningsförlaget Liber AB.

Läroplan för grundskolan 1980 (Lgr 80):, Skolöverstyrelsen, Stockholm: Liber Utbildningsförlaget.

Levy, B. (1972) 'The school's role in the sex-role stereotyping of girls: A feminist review of the literature'. *Feminist Studies,* 1.

National Board of Education (NBE) I 86:74. A study on some activities implemented in Sweden to promote equality of opportunity for girls in technical and vocational education. SÖ Informerar I 86:74 Stockholm: Garnisonstryckeriet: Stencil.

Proposition, Kungl Maj:ts, 1950:70 angående riktlinjer för det svenska skolväsendets utveckling. Stockholm: Riksdagen.

Skolöverstyrelsen (1975) Ett friare val. *Jämställdhetsprogram för skolan.* Rapport från SÖ-projektet Könsrollerna i skolan. Vällingby Liber Läromedel/Utbildningsförlaget.

Spender (1982) *Roles of teachers – what choices do they have? Sex Stereotyping in schools. Council of Europe.* Strasbourg: Stencil.

Stage, C. (1985) *Kvinnliga naturvetare. En motsägelse?* Pedagogisk debatt 20 1979, Umeå universitet. Rapport från pedagogiska institutionen: Stencil.

Statistics Sweden (SCB) (1985) *Women and men in Sweden. Facts and figures. Equal opportunity.* Know your facts 1985. Stockholm: Statistics Sweden.

Statistiska Centralbyrån (SCB) (1986) 'Kvinno- och mans-världen,' *Fakta om jämställdheten i Sverige 1986.* Statistics Sweden, Stockholm: Norstedts.

Svensk Författningssamling (SFS) 1979:1118: *Lag om jämställdhet mellan kvinnor och män i arbetslivet utfärdad den 17 december 1979.*

Ve, H. (1982) Makt, intresse och socialisation. *Kvinnovetenskaplig tidskrift* 2.

Wernersson, J. (1977) *Könsdifferentiering i grundskolan.* Göteborg: Studies in Educational Sciences 1977.

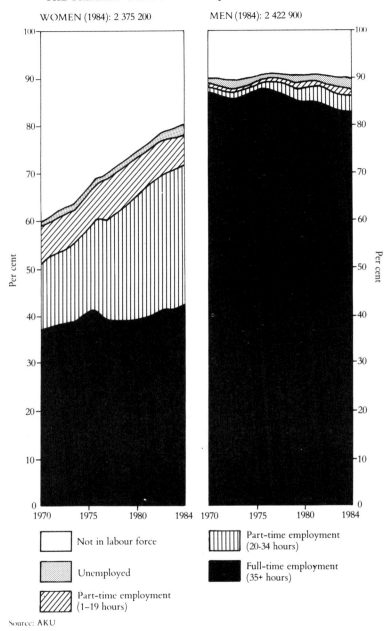

Figure 1 Occupational status of 20- to 64-year-olds in 1970–84.

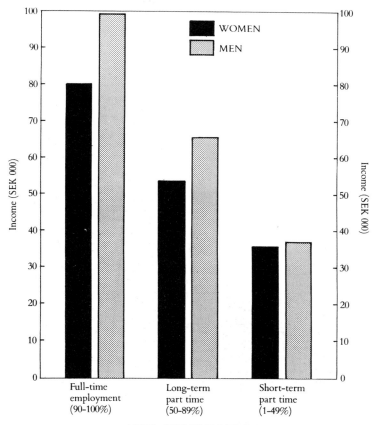

**Employees in the 20–64-year age group
by level of employment 1982**

Level of employment	Women		Men	
	Thousands	%	Thousands	%
Full time (90–100%)	672	41	1432	81
Part time (50–89%)	712	43	215	12
Part time (1–49%)	267	16	118	7
Total	1651	100	1765	100

Source: SA

Figure 2 Earned income by level of employment in 1982 (average for employees aged 20 to 64 years).

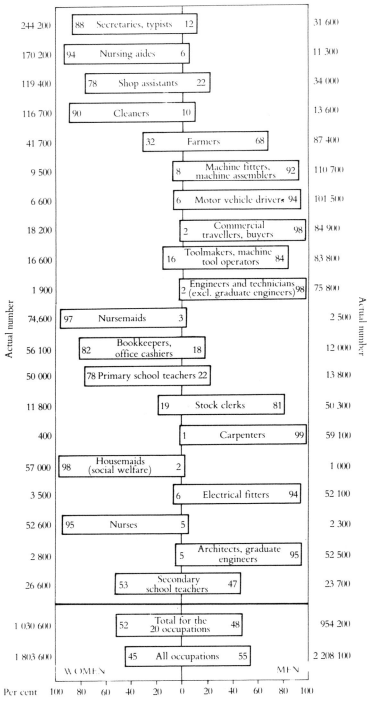

Actual number	WOMEN		MEN	Actual number
244 200	88	Secretaries, typists	12	31 600
170 200	94	Nursing aides	6	11 300
119 400	78	Shop assistants	22	34 000
116 700	90	Cleaners	10	13 600
41 700	32	Farmers	68	87 400
9 500	8	Machine fitters, machine assemblers	92	110 700
6 600	6	Motor vehicle drivers	94	101 500
18 200	2	Commercial travellers, buyers	98	84 900
16 600	16	Toolmakers, machine tool operators	84	83 800
1 900	2	Engineers and technicians (excl. graduate engineers)	98	75 800
74,600	97	Nursemaids	3	2 500
56 100	82	Bookkeepers, office cashiers	18	12 000
50 000	78	Primary school teachers	22	13 800
11 800	19	Stock clerks	81	50 300
400	1	Carpenters	99	59 100
57 000	98	Housemaids (social welfare)	2	1 000
3 500	6	Electrical fitters	94	52 100
52 600	95	Nurses	5	2 300
2 800	5	Architects, graduate engineers	95	52 500
26 600	53	Secondary school teachers	47	23 700
1 030 600	52	Total for the 20 occupations	48	954 200
1 803 600	45	All occupations	55	2 208 100

Per cent 100 80 60 40 20 0 20 40 60 80 100

Figure 3 The twenty most popular occupations in 1980 listed by size.

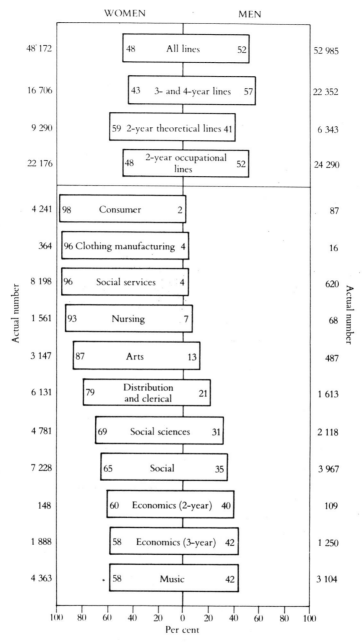

Figure 4 Upper secondary school leavers completing courses in 1982/83 school year.

31

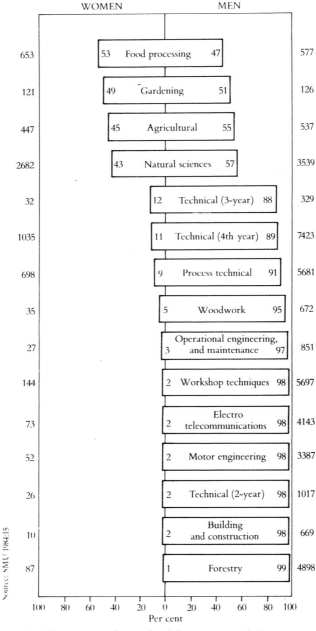

Figure 4 Upper secondary school leavers completing courses in 1982/83 school year.

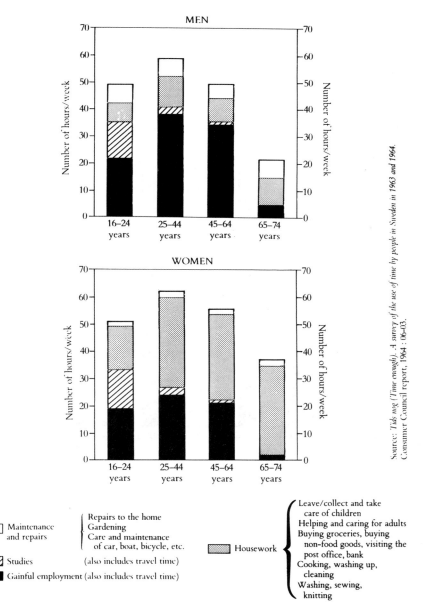

Figure 5 Time use by different age groups (1982–83).

33

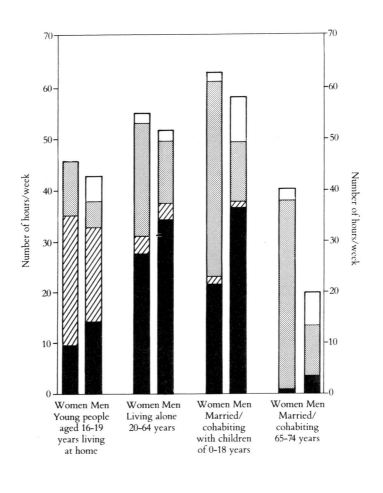

Figure 6 Time use at different stages in the life cycle (1982–83).

CHAPTER 2

Developing Educational Policy on Gender in the Primary School: The Contributions of Teachers in the United Kingdom

Gaby Weiner

My goal in this chapter is twofold; first to provide an indication of the immense diversity of projects and initiatives on gender and education in the United Kingdom since 1975, and second to show how ideas and strategies have developed. In order to make the task more manageable, I shall focus in particular, on the ideas and strategies of *teachers*, and in particular those teachers who were pioneers in the field, and who were active at the end of the 1970s through to the mid-1980s.

While I concentrate on the achievements of teachers, they did not work in isolation. They drew support from several national projects such as *Girls into Science and Technology* (1981–4), and the *Schools Council Sex Differentiation Project* (1981–3), and more recently from the *Genderwatch* materials developed by Kate Myers in Merton (Myers, 1987). Though central government tended to distance itself from emphasis on equality issues (Arnot, 1987), a number of local education authorities were active in promoting sex equality (see Whyte et al., 1985). Teachers also drew on the work of feminist academics such as Valerie Walkerdine who developed theories about shifting power relations in the primary classroom, for instance, between boys and girls, teachers and pupils, and about the complexities of children's learning of gender difference (Walkerdine, 1981). At the same time the teachers' unions began to press for better promotion prospects for women teachers (EOC/NUT, 1980).

Nevertheless, it has been feminist teachers who have provided the main impetus for change. A summary of their achievements can best be shown as a sequence of activities and strategies. These include:

(a) establishing that gender inequalities exist, i.e. defining the 'problem';
(b) initiating changes in school policy and classroom practice, and exploring ways of sustaining progress;
(c) reflecting practically and theoretically on the different kinds of approaches available and on differing priorities; and
(d) implementing more developed equality strategies in schools on the basis of earlier successes and failures.

ESTABLISHING THE EXISTENCE OF GENDER INEQUALITIES

In the first instance, feminist teachers were concerned with raising awareness amongst their colleagues about the extent of gender inequalities in education. They focused on three areas in particular. They considered *attitudes*, both of pupils and teachers, e.g. it was argued that whilst teachers believed that they treated boys and girls without prejudice, detailed investigation showed that this was not the case and that girls appeared to be seriously disadvantaged in the schooling system (Clarricoates, 1978; Spender, 1980; Stanworth, 1981 etc.); *school organization and resources* e.g. inequitable staffing patterns, sex-stereotyping in texts and reading schemes, and sex-specific patterns of subject choice at thirteen plus (see, for instance, Whyld, 1983); and the *activity of women in the labour force*, particularly on the statistical unlikelihood of women remaining in the home for most of their adult lives and the consequent need to change traditional, i.e. domestic-related, career choices of girls (Joshi et al., 1982). For the primary teacher, trying to change *attitudes* and *school organization and resourcing* were clearly of greatest importance. For instance, emphasis was placed on the following features of primary schools:

(a) There were major inequalities in staffing patterns. Although over 80 per cent of primary teachers were women, the headteacher and teacher responsible for science and mathematics were usually men. The school caretaker was invariably male, and the cleaners, secretaries and helpers female.

(b) Textbooks and reading schemes portrayed stereotyped views of family life – white middle-class – and gave mothers and fathers clearly defined and separate roles. The language used in classroom materials was also frequently sexist (and racist).

(c) Where school uniform was required (rather less frequently at primary than at secondary level), girls were compelled to wear skirts and boys trousers.

(d) Teachers tended to give boys more attention and find them more stimulating than girls, yet praise girls for neatness and good behaviour. They also had higher academic expectations of boys and were more likely to attribute poor performance to lack of motivation in boys, and lack of ability in girls.

(e) Whilst most primary-school children attended mixed-sex schools, girls and boys were likely to be taught separately for craft subjects and sport activities. They were also treated differentially on other occasions, for instance, at registration, when lining up to move around the school, and for tasks such as clearing up (girls) or moving PE equipment (boys).

(f) As children progressed through the primary school, their 'free choice' activities and play became increasingly sex stereotyped.

This summary of research indicates the range of issues being considered at primary level. Findings were publicized in a variety of ways – in the form of written or verbal reports to school staff meetings, to school in-service conferences, or to evening seminars arranged by local 'women in education' groups. Feminist teachers also used their findings to lobby advisers and administrators for changes in policy and for practical support, e.g. in providing funding for the production of non-sexist teaching materials.

INITIATING CHANGES

Once the problem of gender inequality had been established, solutions were sought that could be readily injected into school life. *Ad hoc* strategies were developed which included:

- the creation of equal opportunities working parties and posts to devise 'whole school' policies,
- revision of school materials (e.g. texts, reading schemes, examination questions and displays),
- raising awareness about equality issues at staff, parents' and governors' meetings,
- rearranging timetabling to enable pupils to opt more easily for non-traditional subjects such as physics for girls and modern languages for boys,
- appointing female senior staff to provide fresh role models for female pupils,
- encouraging wider career aspirations by inviting people holding non-traditional jobs into school,
- changing school organization by, for instance, 'de-sexing' registers and 'uni-sexing' school uniform.

In addition for primary schools, it was suggested that teachers might:

- encourage pupils to sit and work in *mixed* sex groups;
- share out tasks so that girls are encouraged to do more strenuous and active tasks, and boys asked, for example, to clear up;
- try to consciously give more *time* to the quiet, less-demanding children, usually the girls (though not always);
- choose and adapt stories to redress the sex bias in children's adventure stories and folk tales;
- when making worksheets and classroom resources, use non-sexist language e.g. police officer rather than policeman, and provide a range of positive images of women;
- not assume that the nuclear family is the only acceptable and positive family life style.

The main focus of teachers was upon school-based practical change; how could they help reduce inequalities between the sexes by changing their own and their colleagues' perceptions and practice? Yet the solutions were highly diverse. They stemmed not merely from local or individual school priorities but also from critical differences in the perspectives of the teachers themselves.

REFLECTING ON DIFFERENCES IN APPROACH

By the early 1980s two different feminist teacher perspectives became discernible in the challenge to previous educational practices of gender differentiation and division; the 'equal opportunities' and 'anti-sexist' (or 'girl-centred') approaches (Weiner, 1985).

Briefly the equal opportunities approach aimed at reforms on behalf of girls and women, and sometimes boys and men, within the existing educational structure. The anti-sexist approach aimed at changing unequal power relations between the sexes by transforming the ˙patriarchal and ethnocentric nature of school structures and curricula. These differences became evident in the strategies chosen by teachers to challenge sexist schooling.

The equal opportunities approach emphasized, for instance, persuading girls to develop scientific and technological skills, textbook reform, and at secondary level, changing sex stereotyped subject choices and a common curriculum. It emphasized equal female **representation** in the higher echelons of school and society. Anti-sexist approaches, on the other hand, focused on combining anti-sexist and anti-racist strategies, challenging male school knowledge by considering what '*her*story' or girl-centred science might look like. At upper secondary level they also addressed the more contentious issues of sexuality, sexual harassment, heterosexuality and homophobia. Their concern was that of **empowering** female pupils and teachers in their struggle against the male domination of schooling.

While both approaches were **feminist** in that they wanted to improve educational opportunities for girls and women, they had different priorities for change. Those favouring equal opportunities opted for awareness-raising and consensual change. They asked for increased in-service training as a means of ensuring recognition of sex equality as a professional issue. Anti-sexist teachers, in contrast, focused on more structural changes in their emphasis on the importance of unequal power relations and the need to address conflicting interests. They sought to challenge male domination of schooling by, for instance, establishing schoolgirls' and women's support groups, designing 'girl-centred' curricula and replacing hierarchy, competitiveness and selection with co-operation and democracy. This dual classification has proved helpful in understanding why certain strategies were more attractive to some than others. However, critics (e.g. Acker, 1986) point to the difficulty, in practice, of identifying such clear differences in perspective and strategy. Despite theoretical differences teachers' initiatives crossed the boundaries between the two approaches, and teachers holding different perspectives formed alliances to strengthen their campaigns on behalf of girls and women.

It has become apparent in the past few years that experience of trying to implement change in schooling has brought the two approaches closer together. They have gained from each other and new strategies have emerged which combine features of both.

AN ALLIANCE IN POLICY AND PRACTICE?

Recent strategies, most noticeable in the London area, have modified the two approaches, not for radical change, but for feasible and practical reform. The necessity of majority staff support for the effective implementation of change has led to an emphasis on developing 'whole school' policy on gender. The discovery that it needs more than merely tinkering with timetabling to make girls opt for traditionally male subjects has stimulated deeper thinking about the underlying reasons for gender differentiation. Moreover, acknowledgement of the potential influence of in-service training and of the continued need to raise awareness has led to the creation of a variety of school and authority courses and publications (e.g. ILEA, 1986; Adams and Walkerdine, 1986). These have enabled gender issues to be explored in greater depth by teachers outside the pioneering cohort.

Attention at primary level has now focused on 'whole school' policies (see appendix for some good examples). These have included making changes in school organization to, for instance, reduce boys' domination of the playground, to develop a no-fights policy, to organize *her*story assemblies, and to promote football for both girls and boys. The perceived necessity of addressing both sexism and racism across curricular boundaries has led to a change of emphasis; from 'colour-blind' to 'colour sensitive'. This has led to interest in, for instance, exploring girls' experiences of racism in school as a basis for change, and designing activities specifically to meet the interests of girls from differing ethnic groups.

New ways have been developed of involving parents in equal opportunities work and in the life of the school, and of collaborating with the local community. New methods of classroom management encourage co-operation and respect for others among pupils, rather than competition and inevitably, failure for some. School subjects have been revised to make them more accessible and interesting to girls and black pupils, and sanctions have been threatened against publishers who were slow in eradicating bias from their educational materials (ILEA, 1986).

In surveying the achievements of feminist teachers, whatever their perspective, there have been noticeable gaps. For instance, only recently has any attention been given to how to plan effectively for change (Myers, 1987). There appears to have been a failure to differentiate between short-term and long-term goals – to distinguish between, for instance, the time needed to eradicate sexist comments from texts and that needed to alter pupil or teacher consciousness. Moreover, there have been few attempts to evaluate the achievements of work on gender; perhaps because aims have been overly ambitious resulting, at times, in disappointingly slow progress. Another possible reason is that teacher activists have tended to be women located at the lower levels of school hierarchies who have put all their (limited) energy and influence into achieving recognition of gender equality as an educational aim.

To summarize this paper, I have outlined the development of feminist ideas on educational priorities and their realization. I have described the achievements of the 'pioneer' teachers, their political commitment and their differences of approach. Though the national scene remains patchy, feminist teachers have made substantial progress in legitimizing equal opportunities as a mainstream education issue, particularly where institutional support has been provided by local authorities.

The achievement of feminist teachers has been that, despite lack of commitment and support from central government, few in education in the United Kingdom can now deny that equal opportunities is an important educational issue. Government attacks on local authorities, which provide most of the funding and resources for equal opportunities work, and on teachers, particularly through education legislation (viz. the Educational Reform Act 1988) has, however, placed the future of equal opportunities work in jeopardy. Whether the progress made in the 1980s can be sustained, and even improved upon in the 1990s, is unfortunately a matter of speculation rather than inevitability.

REFERENCES

Acker, S. (1986) 'What feminists want from education', in Hartnett A. and Naish M., (eds) *Education and Society Today*, Falmer.

Adams, C. and Walkerdine, V. (1986) *Investigating Gender in the Primary School*, London: ILEA.

Arnot, M. (1987) 'Political lip-service or radical reform? Central governments responses to sex equality as a policy issue', in Arnot M. and Weiner, G. (eds) *Gender and the Politics of Schooling*, London: Hutchinson.

Clarricoates, K. (1978) 'Dinosaurs in the classroom: a re-examination of some aspects of the hidden curriculum in primary schools', *Women's Studies International Quarterly*, **1**, 4.

Equal Opportunities Commission/National Union of Teachers (1980) *Promotion and the Woman Teacher*, London: EOC.

Inner London Education Authority (1986) *Primary Matters*, London: ILEA.

Joshi, H., Layard, R. and Owen, S. (1982) *Female Labour Supply in Post-war Britain*, London: Centre for Labour Economics.

Myers, K. (ed) (1987) *Genderwatch*, London: EOC/SCDC.

Spender, D. (1980) *Man-made Language*, London: RKP.

Stanworth, M. (1981) *Gender and Schooling: A Study of Sexual Divisions in the Classroom*, London: Hutchinson.

Walkerdine, V. (1981) 'Sex, power and pedagogy', *Screen Education*, **38**.

Weiner, G. (1985) 'Equal opportunities, feminism and girls' education: introduction', in Weiner, G. (ed) *Just a Bunch of Girls: Feminist Approaches to Schooling*, Milton Keynes: Open University Press.

Whyld, J. (ed) (1983) *Sexism and the Secondary Curriculum*, London: Harper and Row.

Whyte, J., Deem, R., Kant, L. and Cruickshank, M. (eds) (1985) *Girl Friendly Schooling*, London: Methuen.

APPENDIX*

Examples of school policies on sex equality

SHAFTESBURY PARK INFANTS SCHOOL

January 1980

Equal opportunities in education

1 *The Sex Discrimination Act of 1975*[1] obliges us as teachers to follow the spirit of the Act in our schools.

2 *The Equal Opportunities Commission* has statutory duties to:

(a) 'work towards eliminating discrimination.'

(Many contraventions of the Act are matters of simple discrimination, often to do with vocational training, and don't apply in an infants school like ours.)

(b) 'promote equality of opportunity between men and women generally.'

The Education and Training Section of the EOC maintain that there are still influences which tend to prevent equality of opportunity and promote stereotyped roles. It is in this subtle area that we need to operate.

3 *The Education and Training Sections* are working to extend teachers' understanding of sex stereotyping, sex role socialisation, and sex discrimination. What follows are some areas for us to consider, mostly based on their suggestions:

4 *Roles*

Young children are very suggestible. They copy the adults they have contact with, and absorb attitudes without our necessarily noticing.

(a) Is there an imaginative play area in the classroom where children can create an environment and develop roles? We usually do offer this. Children are bound to reflect roles that they see in their homes. We can extend their imagination by providing props e.g. dressing up clothes to facilitate girls being astronauts, boys being nurses, and male and female child dolls so that both sexes can be seen to be caring and cared for.

(b) Do our display material and books encourage stereotypes?

*From: Inner London Education Authority, *Primary Matters*, 1986.

43

(c) Are we re-enforcing expectations about roles at home which are unnecessary and out of date?

Do our books etc. always show women cooking and cleaning, and men going to work?

In Shaftesbury Park, as elsewhere, the children's home experience is broader than this (e.g. one-parent families). Does our material reflect real life? Or are there other reasons for including it? We can't and don't wish to reject all literature showing traditional sex roles. Young children learn to read most easily on material that does reflect home experience. But it should be our concern to choose the best of that kind of literature, where roles are not rigid and other values are shown.

At the same time, we do not wish to teach our children that home-making is a lesser occupation than others, which would be to rob the homemaker of the dignity of her/his work.

5 *Different activities for the sexes?*

Of course we don't prevent anyone from doing what they express a wish to do, but could we do more to get children to try new things?

(a) Exam results show that girls under-achieve in maths and science, compared with boys. This may be due to girls' lack of experience with mechanical toys, i.e. a lack of early spatial awareness activities.

Do we encourage girls to use Lego, bricks, train sets, etc? They are available in the classroom but do both sexes make equal use of them?

Teachers who think that the children are not choosing to use the full range of activities provided can arrange the structured parts of the day so that, for example, girls are given Lego to use, or boys are asked to dress the doll up in a specific outfit. This is to be in addition to the free choice time of the day, not instead of it.

(b) The reverse of (a) is the question of whether boys draw, write, and converse as much as girls, and the same action could apply.

(c) Are training and practice in the use of essential tools available to boys and girls? On the whole we think they are, except in the area of playground activities. Do girls kick balls, do boys skip? Girls aren't 'banned' from playtime football, but we should offer the opportunity. They have aggression to release just as boys do.

6 *The Non-Discriminatory Environment*

(a) Obviously school's influence will be limited. But we can try to provide opportunity for the children to discover and develop skills and interests, rather than just accept those traditionally associated with one sex.

(b) We have time and space in our curriculum to investigate issues, e.g. why is it acceptable for girls to cry, but boys think each other babies if they do? A skilled infants' teacher can make her own decisions about when to enlarge a discussion, for example, when a boy in the home corner says, 'I don't wash up'!

(c) Are we providing what the EOC call a non-discriminating environment? There is no need for boys and girls to line up separately. Moving about the building is not a time when we need to emphasise a difference between the sexes. Two lines can be achieved by each taking a partner. Classes can be divided by colour of clothes, date of birthday, initial of name, etc.

(d) Registers and lists can be alphabetical and certainly don't need to be according to sex.

(e) Do boys do all heavy jobs and girls the delicate ones? Do we treat them the same? Is there any difference in strength/delicacy at this age? We need to choose people suitable to tasks, but strong girls are as effective as strong boys at this age.

(f) We also need to remember the example we set by our own behaviour. We are all female teachers in this environment. The only male is the schoolkeeper, who tends to all the fixing and lifting. We need to show co-operation, consideration and self-sufficiency when appropriate.

[1] Sex Discrimination Act (1975) HMSO.

HORNIMAN PRIMARY SCHOOL
EQUAL OPPORTUNITIES (GENDER) POLICY – 1984
General Statement

This school community is opposed to discrimination on the grounds of sex. We believe that such discrimination is contrary to justice and equality, and undermines respect and co-operation amongst individuals within our community. We have developed this policy on the basis of in-school observation in order:

(a)   to promote equality of treatment for all our pupils and staff,

(b)   to ensure that girls and boys receive a fair share of educational resources,

(c)   to implement positive action for girls where necessary, and

(d)   to challenge sex-stereotyping of girls and women, and boys and men.

1 What Is Sexism and What Can Be Done about It?

1.1 *Definition of the problem*

Sexism is the act of regarding and/or treating women and girls as inferior on the grounds of their sex.

We are in agreement with the ILEA Inspectorate Report[1] and the ILEA findings on *Race, Sex and Class*[2] that girls and women are discriminated against in society and that education is not an exception to this. We recognise that both girls and boys are limited by sexist and stereotypical aspects of school life. However, we believe that for girls the processes and effects are different and more serious. At present even the youngest children are usually conditioned to believe that women are less important and less able than men. This has subtle and pervasive consequences for girls and women. These range from individual suffering, such as being subject to sexist abuse and having a low self-regard, to institutionalized discrimination, such as restricted employment opportunities for girls and women.

We recognise too that boys are affected by sex-stereotyping because it restricts the behaviour they learn. It is generally the case that boys are seldom given the opportunity to develop – or even actively discouraged from showing – many abilities we should like to foster in all children. These include: self-sufficiency in domestic needs, e.g. dressmaking, cooking, hygiene; emotional independence; being expressive about their feelings and needs without being demanding; consideration, sensitivity, co-operating with others. Furthermore, boys may be ridiculed for appearing effeminate (e.g. being called a 'cissy'). However, it is because they are being associated with 'feminine' attributes and behaviour, and therefore regarded as inferior, that such insults are degrading. In contrast, the masculine stereotype is almost always regarded as superior, desirable or normal (so calling a girl a 'tomboy' does not have the same connotations of inferiority).

During observation throughout the school it has been evident that sexism and sex-stereotyping pervade the way pupils interact with each other and with teachers and is pervasive also in books and other teaching materials, in the allocation of resources, in the curriculum, in games and play facilities and in many other aspects of school life.

1.2 *What can be done about sexism in the school community?*

We are concerned to broaden sex roles and encourage girls and boys to value and respect themselves, each other and their contribution to school life. We recognise that this is not only a matter of how children see themselves, but also concerns the way that children and adults treat each other. Generally, we would encourage girls to take more initiative, to be more active, adventurous and independent; and boys to be more sensitive, caring, co-operative compassionate and domestically skilled.

2 Dealing with Sexism in the School

2.1 *Organization*

Children should never be deliberately segregated by sex for organizational purposes (e.g. registers, movement about the school, seating and working arrangements, games, etc.).

We do not wish to dictate friendship patterns, but we have sought to encourage girls and boys to play and work together, and we will continue to do this.

However, sometimes it will be necessary to have single-sex groups, e.g. to encourage girls to have a more positive attitude towards subjects such as science and technology; and to encourage boys to value and learn caring and self-help roles.

Children copy the adults they have contact with. Therefore, staff members should share tasks without regard for sex, yet show respect, consideration and care for one another.

This should be borne in mind when allocating tasks to children within school, e.g. errands, librarian duties, book-shop duties, infant playground duties.

2.2 *Attitudes and classroom dynamics*

The Inspectorate Report notes that 'Language is . . . a central force in shaping social attitudes and behaviour'. With this in mind we as a school staff group intend to undertake the following:

i to avoid sexist bias in discussion, writing, description, e.g. use of the word 'mankind', the assumption that all engineers are men, the exclusive use of the pronoun 'he'.

ii to challenge sexist language as used by children and adults, particularly sexist 'jokes' and name-calling.

iii to examine critically:

(a) our expectations of girls' and boys' work, behaviour, life chances and interests, e.g. 'big boys don't cry' and assuming that girls will be interested in 'domestic' subjects.

(b) the nature of reward and punishments, e.g. whether we praise boys more for showing independence and initiative and girls for co-operation and passivity; whether we use a different tone of voice when reprimanding boys or girls.

(c) our responses to assertive behaviour in girls and whether we regard it as unacceptable or inappropriate.

Our observations confirm that, on the whole, boys demand and get more teacher attention that girls. We wish to encourage in girls and boys reasonable assertiveness (as opposed to demanding behaviour) which takes account of other people's space within a group.

3 Teaching for Equality: Resources, Curriculum and Extra-Curricular Activities

3.1 *Resources*

Our observations indicate that girls are reticent about taking their fair share of school resources (teaching materials, equipment, time and space). This may be because boys demand more than their fair share, because staff discriminate (often unconsciously) in favour of boys, or for other reasons. Therefore, we should take steps to reserve girls' fair share for them, and encourage them to take their equal share. Discussion with the children about what we are doing can help to create understanding and alleviate resentment which may be felt by the boys.

i Teaching materials (books, pictures, film strips, video tapes etc.). We intend to carry on building up a stock of teaching materials and storybooks which have positive images of girls and boys in non-stereotyped roles. We will continue to review our present resources critically with the intention of excluding blatantly sexist materials from general use. We may use some of this material for explicit teaching and discussions about sexism.

ii Equipment (games, large apparatus, computer, video-tape machine, video-disc machine, mathematics, and science equipment, constructional equipment and toys). Each child should have equal access to this equipment. Not only does this mean availability to all, but the confidence and training to use it.

iii Time and space

In work and play activities, in the classroom and the playground it is necessary to be vigilant and ensure girls have their equal share of time and space, e.g. girls' use of the enclosed part of the playground.

3.2 *Curriculum and Extra-Curricular Activities*

In educating children, we hope to develop critical awareness of their social and physical environment. As part of this we can use the classroom (and the whole school) itself as a resource to teach about sexism, to dispel myths and develop new ways of learning and of treating each other. This can be developed through:

i Topic Work

(a) Topics should be considered which are particularly appropriate for the study of equal opportunities, e.g. Work, Family, Friends and Caring. Such work should include the children's own observations, tapings and discussions.

(b) Existing topic work should be broadened to include a consideration of women, e.g. 'the Olympics' could be broadened to include how women were originally excluded from the games, how women athletes are now surpassing records made by men in the recent past, and so on.

(c) We need to teach about women's work, experience and history, which has been devalued or even ignored by society. Such topics could include the suffragettes, women at work in the Second World War and women scientists.

(d) We should organise visits by adults in non-stereotyped jobs to talk to children about their work.

ii Opening up the curriculum

(a) We need to make all areas of the curriculum (especially science, mathematics, technology, woodwork, model-making, cooking and needlework) equally accessible and attractive to girls and boys.

We should do this by

— not assuming there are boys' and girls' subjects;

— positive intervention such as organising girls-only groups to play with Lego, solve constructional problems, do a scientific experiment, use the computer.

Having once realised the potential of an activity, and the extent of their own abilities, girls may be less likely to opt out in mixed groups.

Cooking and needlework for boys and girls have traditionally been well catered for in the school and this will continue.

(b) Physical and creative activities. Teachers should try to create situations in which girls and boys have confidence to develop their skills and abilities in physical activities (e.g. games and apparatus). Children should feel free to express their creative talents uninhibited by possible ridicule (e.g. dance and drama).

(c) All children should wear appropriate clothing to school so that they may participate fully and safely in all activities, whether physical, outdoors or messy.

(d) Sex and Health Education: Teachers should encourage children to recognise and accept that men (fathers, other adult men and male siblings) can be involved in the care of babies and young children whether at home or in nurseries, crèches etc.

iii Extra-curricular activities: Every effort should be made to provide a balance of extra-curricular activities so that they are of interest to all children. Activities (e.g. choir, football, netball, softball, swimming, dancing) should be open to boys and girls alike – as are curricular activities – and they should be made to feel welcome by all participants.

iv Parental involvement: Parents, too, provide models for children. We would like to involve more fathers in addition to the mothers coming into school to take groups of young children for various activities (e.g. mothers doing woodwork and fathers doing cooking).

4 In-Service Training

Our policy must be ongoing. We are partly concerned with consciousness-raising among the adults and children of our school, as well as with promoting equality.

Discussions with the community of the school, visits to other schools, the chance to evaluate new materials, and attendance of in-service courses on equal opportunities are essential to the implementation of this policy.

5 Monitoring and Evaluating the Policy

More discussion is needed at various levels in the school from the classroom to the Governing Body, including the staff, parents, children and teachers, on the issues raised in this policy.

We have singled out the following issues for discussion as a priority:
Sexist assumptions in language
Sex equality among the staff of the school
Possible contradictions between this policy and the school's Anti-Racist Policy (e.g. religious and cultural practices which may appear sexist)
Sexual harassment and abuse among staff and children

We need to spend more time observing what goes on in the following areas:
The playground during playtimes
The dining area
Self-chosen activities

The various aspects of school life mentioned previously under Organisation, Attitudes and Classroom Dynamics, Resources, and the Curriculum and Extra-Curricular Activities should also be monitored.

We should keep a record of various incidents, trends and developments observed formally and informally especially as they relate to the effectiveness of positive intervention. We should be able to substantiate our findings with facts and figures.

The results of further observations should be evaluated and discussed by all staff and, where appropriate, children, with a view to developing strategies for positive intervention. These strategies should aim to challenge sexism and promote equality as outlined in the General Statement.

This policy will be regularly reviewed with regard to its effective implementation. If necessary, it should be modified after discussion between the headteacher and representatives from the governors, school staff and Parent Teacher Association.

[1] *Equal Opportunities for Girls and Boys* (1982) A Report by the ILEA Inspectorate. ILEA.

[2] *Race, Sex and Class* 6: *Policy for Equality: Sex* (1985) ILEA Equal Opportunities Unit.

CHAPTER 3

Equality Between Boys and Girls: A Nordic Perspective

Sigrídur Jónsdóttir

This chapter reports on a number of equal opportunities initiatives undertaken by the Scandinavian countries and, in particular, by Iceland. It considers first the influences that cause young children to adopt sex-stereotyped attitudes, for example, the home, the media, children's books and the school. It then describes materials that have been developed for classroom use and in-service programmes designed to raise awareness among teachers about equality issues. Finally, it considers the importance of collaboration between countries, and the relationship between national policy and school practice.

THE PRESENT SITUATION

'Boys are doctors. Girls are nurses,' insisted the kindergarten class. The teacher was aghast that young children could be so firmly entrenched in an anachronism. Persuasion and argument had no effect. The class was firm. Determined to transport these five-year-olds into the 1980s, the teacher took twenty-two youngsters on a field trip to a nearby hospital. She introduced them to a female doctor who talked with them about her job. A male nurse gave them a tour of the hospital.

'What did I tell you?' said the teacher. 'Boys can be nurses. Girls can be doctors.'

'No they can't,' came the riposte.

'What do you mean?' The teacher was stunned. 'We visited the hospital with a man who is a nurse and a woman who is a doctor. You met them. They talked with you.'

'Yes,' chorused the children triumphantly, 'but they lied.'

This anecdote is one of many the American professors and researchers Myra Sadker, David Sadker and Susan Klein (1986, p. 121) recounted after they travelled round the United States, talking to educators, parents and students. The fact that these children were only five to six years old and already had such fixed ideas about sex roles leaves us with the vital question of how they acquired such set ideas. Since they were kindergarteners, school does not seem yet to have been their main arena for developing sex-role identification, though it will loom large as they grow older. The question of origins therefore continues: home? friends? the media? And why were they so determined, even after they had heard and seen the evidence, to cling to their preconceptions.

When children start school at five or six years of age they have already developed a self-image, weak or strong. A part of that self-image is their identification with sex roles. If we look first at the *home*, we must take into account the fact that, from an early age, parents to a large extent treat their sons differently from their daughters. Children are given toys that members of that culture consider appropriate to the sex in question. Boys and girls are given different tasks to do, and books are chosen based on the child's sex.

Researchers have shown that certain concepts underlie the definition of each sex and these concepts form the basis for parental behaviour toward, and expectations of, that sex, boy or girl. Girls, for example, are identified with dependency, passivity, caution, shyness, obedience, helplessness; boys with courage, strength, daring, tolerance, security, independence.

After children learn that a person is either female or male and what that is supposed to mean, they too begin to fall into the pattern that supposedly belongs to one gender or the other. They notice who does what in their family. Believing that what they observe in their home holds true for everybody, they internalize and generalize what they observe and thus learn how to behave themselves. They expand their understanding by listening to the way people talk about certain human characteristics.

What is learned at home is tested and defined by what is experienced in the neighbourhood. Children's assumptions about proper sex roles are strengthened by the seemingly universal acceptance of the same attitudes all round them, and by their desire to be like the other children in the neighbourhood.

Today, even for young children, another potent factor, both within and outside of the home, is the *media*. The power of television to influence children's attitudes begins early and remains a force throughout their formative years. Many children are exposed to a steady stream of programmes that constantly reinforce stereotyped views of men and women. Even, or perhaps especially, in cartoons the characters behave the way females and males are traditionally supposed to behave. Women are rarely shown as having equal power or prestige to men. When children watch programmes with their parents they cannot help but notice that the majority of important people in the news are men. The advertisements on television also underscore the stereotyped male and female statuses.

The *books* read to young children are another important influence in the socialization process. They tend to show boys and men as more likely to be active, clever, willing to take risks, leading more interesting lives, and able to cope effectively with problems, whereas girls are rarely given anything interesting or exciting to do. Beatrix Potter's wonderful *Peter Rabbit* continues to be read for the fun Peter had, even though he was 'bad', and hardly for the 'good' but boring lives his three sisters led. In the same way, fairy tales reinforce the stereotyped views of females and males, where the young man is usually adventurous, brave and strong, but the young woman is presented as the passive prize whose beauty, patience, and trusting nature are her main attributes.

All this inundation from parents and home, neighbourhood acquaintances, television, and books contributes to the building of the child's self-image. Socialization may begin at birth, with pink and blue to differentiate the sexes, and continue through adolescence, when different educational and occupational goals are offered. And as social institutions in general support the idea that boys and girls should be prepared for different adult roles, parents are likely to rely on child-rearing methods that support rigid sex-role divisions.

As the child grows up, *school* is the most important social institution in the development of the child. Is there sexual equality in schools? By law, yes, at least in the Nordic countries, but what about in reality? By law girls and boys, women and men, are promised equal opportunities in relation to life, education, vocational training, and so on. Both girls and boys take such subjects as sewing, domestic science and woodwork, subjects that were traditionally reserved for one sex but are now taught to boys and girls together. But still there is sex discrimination in most schools, I dare say in most countries. Many researchers show that different qualities are emphasized depending upon the sex of the student, many of the same qualities we have met before: girls should be dependent, reserved, obedient, cautious, and submissive while boys should be strong, courageous, daring, and independent.

We also know from research that boys not only receive more attention and encouragement than do girls but also more help. The usual pattern is that girls take up forty per cent of the teacher's time and boys sixty per cent. Most of those in remedial education are boys. One can say that sex-role stereotypes creep into the school throughout the entire day, in one form or another. Many teachers, however unconsciously, continue to use, or are assigned by the school system, teaching methods and materials that are sex-biased and clearly lead to the reinforcement of discrimination based on stereotyped attitudes and sex-role models.

In my country, Iceland, for example, the schools are still using such materials without being aware of it. For example, some textbooks in Icelandic contain stories where boys play the leading roles. In textbooks generally more examples show boys solving difficult problems, whereas girls are often shown in service roles or even as helpless in some situations. The organization of the school itself further reinforces sex-role stereotyping. Most of the primary school teachers today are women, in Iceland as elsewhere, but eighty per cent of the head teachers are men. The children's inevitable conclusion is that girls become teachers and boys become head teachers or school principals.

WHAT CAN BE DONE?

A woman's education must . . . be planned in relation to man. To be pleasing in his sight, to win his respect and love, to train him in childhood, to tend him in manhood, to counsel and console, to make his life pleasant and happy, these are the duties of woman for all time, and this is what she should be taught while she is young. (Rousseau, 1762/1974, p. 328.)

Rousseau's was the message of his time. Furthermore, it is a message that has lasted for an uncommonly long time, and interestingly he, too, recognized that for the indoctrination to be effective it would have to start *early*. We still live with powerful early forces that create different sex roles for boys and girls and these forces might make it seem too late to try to equalize opportunities once the children enter school.

However, people grow and change throughout their lives, and schools are in a position to exert a strong positive influence. Attitudes about sex roles *can* be introduced and changed at any educational level, but the earlier the process is begun the less time children have to become rigid in their beliefs and the less re-education is necessary. Teachers *can* contribute to changing children's views of themselves and to awakening their self-awareness as a first phase toward developing self-identity. They can help children become more aware of the results of sex-role stereotyping and of the variety of forces that influence attitudes, thinking, and behaviour in general and toward sex roles in particular.

Are teachers and other educators really capable of doing this? I believe that teacher awareness is an essential precondition. In this respect, the teacher's education is fundamental, including both pre- and in-service training.

Courses for teachers where self-evaluation is emphasized are important first steps. Teachers must first work with and recognize their own self-awareness – their opinions, feelings and attitudes, before they can help others to the same awareness. For those who are alive to their own feelings and attitudes and to the sex discrimination that so commonly surrounds us these words are a reminder. Others may be at the starting point, just beginning to realize that something is wrong.

When I was teaching I was not aware of any discrimination at my school, I never thought about it, but now I can see it almost everywhere. It depends on the teacher's awareness and attitudes as to whether he or she is able to:

- Help children become more aware of sex-role stereotyping and of the variety of forces that influence attitudes, thinking, and behaviour.

- Change school practices that contribute to the separation and stereotyping of children by gender.
- Help children see that sex-role definitions change with time and vary in different cultures.
- Help children understand that there is a difference between sex roles and gender identity.
- Encourage children to learn to work and play together and experience a variety of roles within a group.'

(Shapiro, 1981, p. 81).

Change is not an event but a process. No change occurs if there is no need felt for it. Changes within the school – in curriculum, materials, methods – mean that the whole school staff must work together. One of the findings from the many case studies on 'Innovation in Primary Education', which make up the *Council of Europe's Project No. 8* (1987, p. 146), is that 'If an innovation is going to be successful, it is important that the whole school staff is motivated for the innovation.' And again, 'The head of the school plays a leading role in all school innovations' (p. 146).

A change towards equal treatment of the sexes concerns both school organization and the work done in school, both parents and school authorities. It is, therefore, very important that *all* the teachers and heads are motivated to deal with sexual equality. Reinforcing this motivation should be a part of all teacher-training courses and workshops.

There is a crying need to analyse and revise the teaching material now in use, and the authors of new materials *must* be made aware of the lasting effect of the stereotyping found in current books and other materials. The problem is twofold: women need to be given credit for their achievements outside the home and the value of housework skills should not be denigrated but given the recognition they are due. For example, authors of history texts should pay attention to women's contributions to cultural achievements as well as to the home, and the traditional responsibilities and skills required in childbearing and childrearing. Running a home has not only been important in the past, but remains important and, will continue to be so. Textbooks must also document women's efforts to break out

57

of their traditional sphere of the home in a way that highlights women's as well as men's activities as historically significant.

We have to become aware of the degree to which the language and expressions we use are themselves sexist, and material used in social studies must deal with the meaning of values and concepts such as self-confidence, leadership, emotional sensitivity, decision-making, empathy, and pro-social behaviour as important skills for all individuals regardless of sex.

One necessity is to involve parents through the teachers, through their children, through the media. We have to find ways to do this, for example by publishing materials for parents and for the media, by inviting parents to conferences and meetings, and by producing films and videotapes.

Special material on sexual equality is also important, both for teaching and as a basis for discussion at workshops for teachers and at parents' meetings. One example of such educational material, written by an author for primary schools, is entitled *Girls and Boys, Equal Individuals* and was published in Iceland in 1985 by the Icelandic Educational Centre. The material consists of forty slides, a teacher's manual, and worksheets for the children, and is divided into four parts:

I. The Family
II. The School
III. Work
IV. Free Time and the Media

Each of these four parts (of ten slides each) has two slides with questions and worksheets that relate to these questions. The manual gives suggestions for various activities for the children in connection with the worksheets, e.g. studies, evaluation, interviews, homework.

This series of slides was produced with the following aims in mind:

• that boys and girls both should look on themselves as equals;
• that children should be aware of their self-image with regard to their appearance, attitudes and emotions. Each child should understand that his/her self-image with regard to his/her sexual role is developed early and should be aware of the factors that influence that image.

The material is based on the following research findings:

- that children's attitudes towards their sexual roles are developed early;
- that children's attitudes towards their sexual roles are formed at home, at school, from their friends, and from the media, etc;
- that in bringing up girls, the following qualities are emphasized: being considerate, protective, tidy and caring, as well as dependent, reserved, shy, obedient, cautious, and submissive;
- that in bringing up boys the following are emphasized: strength, courage, independence, self-assurance, endurance and daring;
- that people are aware of prejudice with regard to the sex roles of boys and girls;
- that girls receive less attention and encouragement in school than boys;
- that boys not only receive more attention and encouragement in school than girls but also more help;
- that women's education and work is less valued by society and less well remunerated than men's. Apart from this, it is largely only women who carry out the unpaid work of, for example, running the home and bringing up children;
- that girls less often apply for technical jobs, or advanced work in the field of computer science.

This material can be used over a long period and is preferably used in connection with social studies, language teaching, or other subject areas. It has, at the time of writing, been used for two years in many Icelandic primary schools. The problems in the beginning were made clear from comments from the teachers, as the following examples illustrate:

(a) Six-year-old children were drawing pictures and telling the teacher what they wanted to do when grown up. The boys volunteered: 'I want to be a pilot, a policeman, a banker, a football player, a bus driver, a ship's captain', and so on, whereas almost all the girls wanted to take care of children. There is also a great difference in how the boys and girls described their play.

(b) Nine-year-old children were filling out worksheets describing themselves. The boys' self-image was much more positive than that of the girls'. The boys indicated 'I *am* good at football, I *am* strong, I *am* clever, I *can* swim well', for example, while the girls gave more cautious replies, such as 'I *think* I can do this or that well', or they complained about their appearance.

(c) Twelve-year-old children worked with this material off and on for the whole school year. They completed many studies in the classroom; for example, they answered the questions 'What would you like to be?' and 'What would you like to be if you were the opposite sex?' About 50 per cent of the children chose something else to be if they had been the opposite sex.

The entire staff of each school participated in a workshop for two days in November prior to using the material and then made use of it throughout the school year. The staff then held another workshop for one day to share experiences and discuss the results of using this material.

In the summer of 1987 a group of Icelandic teachers attended a five-day in-service training programme. The principal emphasis was on developing teacher self-awareness and self-evaluation, and the realization that there is a progression from self-awareness to self-identity. The teachers were shown that to succeed in leading children to develop an effective self-identity they must first do so themselves.

The second part of the programme was devoted to introducing the new material described above and showing different ways of using the material. Part of the training was to teach strategies for asking questions and holding discussions.

The third part of the programme consisted of group work analysis of various textbooks and other teaching materials, in connection with a workshop where the teachers themselves produced materials and shared ideas about helpful resources.

One afternoon session consisted of an open meeting (announced in advance in the newspapers) on sex equality in schools to which we invited qualified people in education to lecture and take part in a panel discussion. During the training programme we also had one or two lectures on such topics as recent research results, sexist language, and sex-stereotyping in literature.

The most important part of the course, however, was a one-day follow-up meeting held two months later, at which we were able to share experiences.

NORDIC CONFERENCES ON SEX EQUALITY

For many years there has been close co-operation between the
Nordic countries of Denmark, Finland, Iceland, Norway and
Sweden in matters pertaining to education and cultural events.
This co-operation is organized by the Nordic Council of Minis-
ters, with head offices in Copenhagen. One aspect of this co-
operative effort concerns sexual equality.

In the autumn of 1985, the Council initiated a 'Break-through
Project', to run for a period of four years, in order to develop
various models for breaking through the sexually segregated
labour market. As a joint Nordic project there is follow-up
research in all the five countries to see how the girls who have
chosen non-traditional education have made out. The Council
is also responsible for other projects, including one on women
in the decision-making process. A handbook on women in
politics was published in the summer of 1987 by the Nordic
Council.

A conference on 'Sex Roles in Schools' was held in Copenhagen in December, 1984. The main conclusions and recommendations of this conference were that:

(a) The Council should make proposals about sex equality
     in education in both pre- and in-service training of all
     teachers.
(b) The Nordic countries should invite teachers to five-day
     courses which would prepare them to be leaders in sexual
     education in their school districts.
(c) The Council should be encouraged to publish both
     informative and provocative debating materials for
     parents.
(d) The Nordic Council should influence the debate on edu-
     cation and the labour market by focusing more on the
     resource potential of women's intelligence, e.g. in new
     technologies.
(e) The Council should lead this continuing co-operation
     because of the great importance of having scientists, edu-
     cators, and administrators co-operating to resolve the
     problems of equality for the sexes.
(f) The Council should initiate a Sex Equality Year in all
     schools in the five countries.

Another Nordic conference on sex equality in schools and

teacher education, entitled 'A Girl and a Boy: Equal Position', was held in Copenhagen from 15 to 17 September 1987. The Council invited eight delegates from each country, representing three main groups: teachers, researchers, and administrators. The main objective of this conference was to define ways to make teachers aware of sex discrimination and the potential for sex equality, and to integrate such steps into all teacher training. The following topics were covered in lectures and group work:

- The present situation as regards sex equality in the Nordic countries.
- Teacher-pupil awareness of the problem.
- Language and behaviour at school.
- Content and teaching methods in science and learning about new technologies.
- Strategies to implement sex equality education.

There were five workshops, one for each country. The conference also included an exhibition of teaching materials, books, posters, slides, videotapes, films, and other materials.

At the conclusion of the conference, a joint resolution was prepared to send to the Nordic Council of Ministers. The resolution presented seven proposals for action to be taken in the next few years. The first proposal, together with the accompanying explanatory statement, was that:

(a) 1990 shall be declared the Year of Sexual Equality in the primary schools in all the Nordic countries.

The data that has been presented at the conference has shown that people make a special effort to right the imbalance if sexual equality is increased in the schools.

Boys should not be able to get ahead at the expense of girls, as is now the case. The conference participants feel that, if sexual equality is to become a fact in society, it is necessary to make an effort in the primary schools where awareness and stereotyping of sex roles is formed. It is necessary to change the schools so that girls have a chance to learn and gain experience. Additionally, girls must have increased opportunities to choose education and jobs on an equal footing with the boys such that women have increased opportunities in the job market.

The other proposals were that:

(b) There should be co-operation between the Nordic countries to bring about sex equality in teacher training.

(c) Research on sex equality in the primary schools and continuing education should be strengthened in the Nordic countries.

(d) All relevant work in progress in the Nordic countries should be recorded.

(e) An agency should be founded to collect and distribute information about research on and progress in bringing about sex equality in the schools and in teacher training.

(f) In 1989 a Nordic conference should be held to continue the work begun at this conference.

(g) The Nordic Council of Ministers should work for equal hiring practices in all management, councils, and committees that concern the primary schools and teacher training.

But these proposals, important as they are, are only plans. We are combating an old tradition – attitudes and feelings that it may take years to change. Nevertheless, we *have to try*. We have to change attitudes and opinions and deep-seated values. Jobs dealing with education, caring, and human relations, for example, are not less important than counting money in a bank. We have to prepare our children for adult responsibilities where women and men must work co-operatively, as parents, in the workforce, in international relations, and as citizens. In the words of Scott (1986, p. 248), 'Our society needs females who can lead, males who can nurture, and individuals who accept each other as equals.'

If we succeed, our children at six will no longer be able to say: 'Yes, but they lied.'

REFERENCES

Harvey, G. and Hergert, L. (1986) 'Strategies for achieving sex equity in education', in *Theory into Practice, Sex Equity and Education*, The Ohio State University.

Jones, D. and Wilkins, W. (1986) 'Sex equity in parenting and parent education', in *Theory into Practice, Sex Equity and Education*, The Ohio State University.

Jónsdóttir, S. (1985) *Stelpur, strákar, jafngildir einstaklingar*, Námsgagnastofnun, Reykjavik.

Jónsdóttir, S. (1987) 'Project No. 8 on Innovation in Primary Education', Final Report, DECS/EGT. *Case Studies on Innovations*, Council of Europe.

Ligestillingsrådet (1986) *Årsberetning*, Copenhagen.

Nordisk Ministeråd (1985) *Kön og roller i skollen*, Copenhagen.

Sadker, D., Sadker, M. and Klein, S. (1986) 'Abolishing misperceptions about sex equity in education', in *Theory into Practice, Sex Equity and Education*, The Ohio State University.

Scott, K. (1986) 'Learning sex equitable social skills', in *Theory into Practice, Sex Equity and Education*, The Ohio State University.

Shapiro, J., Kramer, S. and Hunerberg, C. (1981) *Equal Their Chances. Children's Activities for Non-Sexist Learning*, Prentice-Hall, Englewood Cliffs, NJ.

Spender, D. (1983) *Invisible Woman: The Schooling Scandal*, Writers' and Readers' Publishing Co-operative, London.

Stanworth, M. (1984) *Gender and Schooling. A Study of Sexual Divisions in the Classroom*, 2nd ed., Hutchinson, London.

CHAPTER 4

Sex Equity – The Ontario School Curriculum with Specific Reference to the Role of the Primary Grades

Carole-Anne Bennett

INTRODUCTION

This chapter describes recent strategies adopted by the Ontario Government to promote equal opportunities or 'bias-free learning environments' in schools. It focuses on how equal opportunities policies have developed in Ontario, the thinking behind them, and the particular policies relating to science and the provision of activity-based materials currently in operation. The Ontario Government is committed to the establishment of learning environments in Ontario schools that will encourage each student to develop the knowledge, skills and attitudes necessary for a self-fulfilling and independent life style.

At the time of writing, Ontario's primary/junior programme priorities and teaching strategies are in process of renewal. A clear emphasis on the creation of bias-free learning environment is evident in two policy documents recently developed as part of this renewal process. These documents demonstrate new strategies for influencing teachers in their responsibility for creating bias-free learning environments in the child's early years of school.

The first strategy is to influence teachers' attitudes by increasing their confidence in a subject area, for example, in science. A twenty-four-point *Action Plan* designed to renew the teaching of science in kindergarten through to grade six was developed by the Ministry of Education in 1986. This plan recognizes that girls require encouragement to develop and pursue an interest in studying science.

The draft programme policy document for science, developed as part of the *Action Plan* sets out clear expectations for teachers. It stresses the need for enthusiastic teacher involvement in all science activities in the early grades. In-service programmes are planned to build teacher confidence in the teaching of science topics.

Primary teachers, who are mostly women, frequently do not have a background in science and may provide a stereotypic role model for young children in their presentation of science activities. It is the expectation of the Ministry of Education, that teachers will change their attitudes towards a subject if they become confident and interested in the subject area. This, in turn, will have a direct and positive impact on the interest and response of students to the learning experiences of the subject. In this instance, the subject is science. Overall, the government has committed several millions of dollars to this project.

The second strategy is to force the use of bias-free teaching strategies in classrooms by providing teachers in primary/junior grades with attractive and directly applicable activity-centred work units that are completely bias-free. *Ages 9 through 12*, developed by the Ontario Public School Teachers' Federation and the Ministry of Education to support primary/junior programme priorities in all subject areas, illustrates the expanded philosophy of sex equity in Ontario schools. The illustrations, format and language of this document set up models of learning activities that include 'everyone as an equal'. The pursuit of success as part of one's personal development and growth is viewed as a natural expectation for each child.

This document has had an excellent reception in the schools. Teachers are making direct use of the lessons and activities. The document forces equality in the style and presentation of its learning activities.

Other supportive activities include affirmative action/equal opportunity programmes within local school boards. In 1986, the Ministry of Education introduced an 'Affirmative Action/Employment Equity Incentive Fund'. Financial assistance is provided to school boards to enable them to hire an affirmative action co-ordinator who will monitor affirmative action programmes and initiatives available to its staff. This fund links affirmative action programmes, the role models it can initiate in school and the quality of student learning environments. Most publicly supported schools have taken advantage of this assistance.

With its first statement of a formal sex equity curriculum policy in 1975, the Ministry of Education began to define the role that schools would play in the achievement of equal opportunities for women in Ontario. Over a decade later, in 1988, curriculum sex equity policy addresses both the *quality* and the *equality* of educational opportunities provided for female students in publicly supported elementary and secondary schools.

THE CONTEXT

There are 161 publicly supported school boards in Ontario, 3,723 elementary schools and 764 secondary schools. (This does not include schools for the trainable retarded or care and treatment facilities.) There are 1,166,114 elementary school students and 616,425 secondary students. In addition, there are approximately 549 private schools (elementary, secondary or combined elementary and secondary) with 66,728 students.

The Ministry of Education is responsible for establishing curriculum policies for Ontario schools. These policies are set out in publications called circulars, curriculum guidelines and primary/junior programme policy documents. Together, they define a common framework for curriculum and diploma requirements across the province.

Curriculum policies and programme requirements in Ontario schools ensure an age-appropriate scope and sequence in the learning process. Teachers are expected to work in ways that fit into the natural growth and development stage of the learner. Ontario's sex equity policy supports the belief that the message of individual equality and freedom to grow and develop in accordance with one's potential interests, aptitudes and abilities must be passed on through images, language and daily routines of the school as well as through the programme. Children are conscious of differences between actions and words. Teacher behaviour has a powerful influence on student attitudes.

CURRICULUM POLICY

As I have already mentioned, in 1975 a curriculum sex equity policy was formally introduced to the primary and junior grades in Ontario's elementary schools. The policy statement, although brief, emphasized the commitment of the Ontario Government to the delivery of educational services that would provide each child with the opportunity to develop abilities and aspirations without the limitations imposed by sex-role sterotypes.

This statement of policy was expanded in 1979 for Ontario's secondary schools (i.e. grades 9 to 13). No student could be denied access to any course or programme in a secondary school on the basis of sex. A student's right of access to any educational programme in an Ontario school and the avoidance of sex-role stereotyping in all classrooms was thus established.

A major review of secondary school programmes in the province expanded sex-equity policy to a philosophy of equality that involved the total school learning environment:

> The philosophy of sex equity should permeate all aspects of the school's curriculum, policies, teaching methods and materials, and assessment procedures as well as the attitudes and expectations of its staff and all of its interaction with students, parents and the community.

In addition, it stressed the importance of a curriculum that accurately reflects the experiences and contributions of women in society.

This commitment to sex equity, appropriately tailored, is clearly set out in all subject-related policy documents. For example, science emphasizes the importance of role models for young women relative to their career aspirations, and the need for teachers to analyse their own attitudes and expectations for possible stereotyping in their treatment of boys and girls in science.

The importance of full participation by both boys and girls in science activities and the importance of all teachers consciously demonstrating an interest and involvement in the teaching of science in their classrooms is emphasized.

In support of these policy commitments, all materials approved for school use by the Ministry of Education must be free from racial, ethnic, religious and cultural discrimination, sex bias, bias towards the aged, the handicapped, persons in certain occupations, or individuals belonging to a specific group. School boards and teachers' federations have also developed criteria for assessing bias-free learning materials.

These criteria are judiciously applied in schools. They are also applied to computer software programs, films and video productions. Ontario teachers' federations, professional subject organizations, other government agencies and industrial groups have all been involved in the development of resource documents, pamphlets, special activities and initiatives designed and tailored to assist school administrators and teachers' creation of bias-free learning environments.

The development of sex equity *resources* has closely paralleled the expansion of sex-equity curriculum policies. It is reassuring to know that girls in the elementary schools and young women in the secondary schools of Ontario are receiving the encouragement and support needed to explore freely all aspects of their school curriculum and learning environments.

CONCLUSIONS

Ontario now has the curriculum policies and resources in place that should encourage individual students to pursue educational successes in their chosen areas of interest.

The translation of curriculum policy into effective practice, however, remains dependent on the conscientious commitment of teachers and school administrators to change old and frequently entrenched attitudes, routines and systems. Surface changes, made to meet policy requirements, are not sufficient to ensure quality and equality in the education of all children.

Even with supportive government legislation, sex equity policy remains primarily a women's issue in Ontario. Sex equity in reality is 'education equity', a real issue for all educators. We cannot afford to ignore the realities of the 1980s and 1990s. We need to provide Ontario's young people with equal opportunities to develop their interests, aptitudes and abilities so that they will be able to pursue a personally fulfilling life-style.

PART 2

NATIONAL CASE STUDIES OF EQUAL OPPORTUNITIES: THE EUROPEAN PICTURE

CHAPTER 5

Spain

by the Colectivo Feminista a Favor de las Niñas

In seeking to identify the most important issues relating to sexism and sex inequality in Spanish education, this chapter examines the following areas: the structures and inequalities of the Spanish education system; aspects of education which most affect girls and women; and the progress that has been made in challenging sex inequalities by feminists working inside and outside institutional frameworks.

A DESCRIPTION OF THE SCHOOL SYSTEM IN RELATION TO SEX DISCRIMINATION

Before 1970, schools in Spain were segregated. Boys' schools and girls' schools had separate buildings and, in some cases, different curricula.

In 1970, the General Law of Education was passed (4/1970–7 August). This law was a step forward since it established compulsory and free education for both sexes from six to fourteen years of age, leaving the door open for schools to become mixed. This law affected the whole of the country. Under it two types of school coexisted:

- state schools: free except for school materials (textbooks, notebooks, etc.);
- private schools, some of which were subsidized by the government.

Although the new law defined itself as 'coeducational', it contained explicitly differentiated activities for boys and girls.

The organization of school levels was (and still is) as follows:

Pre-primary Education (from nought to six years of age): non-compulsory and free for 4-5-year-olds only where such pro-

73

vision exists. There are also special schools for this age level called 'guarderias', 'escuela de parvulos' and 'parvulario'. Since these are neither compulsory nor free, women (m s, grandmothers . . .) have to take care of the children who remain at home. Once again, the job of, and responsibility for, child care falls on the adult women of the family.

Education General Basica (Primary School) (six to fourteen years of age): compulsory for all children and free both in state and in subsidized private schools.

In addition, in 1983, a structure of Teachers' Centres was set up. This replaced the system whereby teacher education was the responsibility of the universities. At the same time, teacher education (or in-service training) came under the authority of the Ministry of Education. The purpose of these centres is to speed up and decentralize teacher education. However, the centres have been given masculine names (i.e. Centros de Profesores) and the management posts are held mainly by men. Moreover, all meetings take place after school which women teachers, a vast majority of whom are also housekeepers and mothers, find difficult to attend.

During the school year 1983– the Experimental roject for the Reform of the School System was started. This project took the stance that sexism could be eliminated from schooling only where groups of women teachers who were aware of and sensitive to the issues, submitted concrete proposals. It continued for three years and has now been replaced by a wider-ranging project which we shall refer to later.

In 1985 the Organic Law on the Right to Education (LODE) was passed in the national Parliament. This law advocates non-discrimination on the grounds of sex, but only a p ple. The law, however, opened up ways of community participation in the running of the schools, i.e. through Schools' Councils, where teachers, pupils and parents are represented: 'profesores, alumnos y padres'. Unfortunately, the wording of all documents issued by the Ministry of Education is invariably in the masculine.

In this same year (1985), a decree was issued making all state schools mixed, though private and subsidized schools were not affected by the decree. Two years later, in 1987, the Ministry of Education established the Project for the Reform of University Curricula. Sadly, the project did not include an end to the problem of sex discrimination as one of its aims.

AN ANALYSIS OF THE PARTICULAR ASPECTS OF THE EDUCATION SYSTEM WHICH AFFECT WOMEN

The Teachers

During the years of teacher training, sexism in education is one issue which is not examined. Neither is the variable sex/gender considered as a basis for understanding how the system of education works. For instance, as we show later, the sex of the teacher has a significant influence on which sector or level of schooling he or she works in.

Kindergarten

Until the end of 1970, vacancies in state schools at this level could only be taken up by women and the vast majority of teachers at this level are still women (94 per cent). There are thus hardly any men teachers at kindergarten level and parents are still rather surprised to find one at their child's school. In addition, their expectations of men teachers are different from their expectations of women teachers, being much influenced by existing sex stereotypes.

Primary and Secondary Schooling

Here, most of the teachers are women: 80 per cent at the first stage (six to eight years). This percentage goes down for older pupils, becoming as low as 46 per cent in the Secondary School (post-fourteen). On the other hand, management posts are usually held by men (e.g. Principal, Director of Studies), despite the fact that women teachers are in the majority.

As for the distribution of teachers according to different subject areas, whilst there is no specific ruling on the matter, women tend to be encouraged to specialize in teaching Spanish or history. Men, on the other hand, are offered teaching posts in science and technology as well as responsibility for groups where disciplinary problems are anticipated and a 'strong hand' is required.

The Language

There are four officially recognised languages in Spain: Castilian, Catalan, Galician and Basque. The teaching of Castilian is compulsory in all schools. The other three languages are taught in their respective geographic areas.

The Castilian language, like all languages derived from Latin, has a series of rules regarding the use of gender in grammar. Those most important to concerns about sexism are as follows:

(a) the masculine gender is considered all-embracing, which in practice means that it is used in the plural when referring to a mixed-sex group e.g. 'los alumnos deben. . .' It is also used in the singular when referring to individuals undifferentiated by sex e.g. 'el nino (child), el profesor (teacher), el padre, el alumno' (pupil). The feminine gender is only used to emphasize a specific aspect from which men are excluded – for example, in the case of the teacher asking 'las ninas' (the girls) to stay and decorate the classroom, and 'las limpiadoras' (cleaning staff) not to clean the blackboard;

(b) the uneven balance in the positive/negative implications of words having both masculine and feminine meanings e.g. 'verdulero' (fruit-and-vegetable seller) and 'verdulera' (a vulgar woman): 'alcalde' (mayor) and 'alcaldesa' (the mayor's wife);

(c) the 'patriarchal' definitions of certain words by the *Dictionary of the Royal Academy* (the highest recognized authority in the use of the Castilian language). For instance, the synonyms of 'hombre' (man) are listed as 'varon' (male) and 'persona' (person). Compare these with the listed synonyms of 'mujer' (woman) which are 'conyuge' (spouse) and 'puta' and 'ramera' (whore). The educational system transmits and reinforces these rules without even questioning the way they affect the identity of girls and boys taking part in the educational process or in which they inhibit pupils' capacity to symbolize, express and communicate;

(d) the wording of school documents in the masculine. There are only 'ninos, profesores, directores, padres, tutores' though there are exceptions e.g. 'mujeres de la limpieza' (cleaning women);

76

(e)   the wording of oral expression is similarly in the masculine;
(f)   the transmission of linguistic rules and norms as unquestionable and unchangeable in relation to their undoubted sexist implications;
(g)   in single sex schools where there are only girl pupils and women teachers, the masculine gender is nevertheless often used in speech and documents (e.g. 'los profesores deben', 'la educacion de los ninos es').

Teaching Materials

There is no clear, specific policy about the publication and use of teaching materials. The Ministry of Education has a somewhat non-committal attitude to the subject. Textbooks, videos, cassettes, software, games and other teaching resources therefore remain sexist.

Teachers decide on the materials to be used in the classroom. If they become aware of the sexism in their materials, they can either design their own material (which is likely to create considerable extra work) or use the existing material in such a way as to make students/pupils critically aware of its nature.

Grouping of Pupils in Schools

Unless teachers intervene, boys and girls will reproduce existing social models and cultures voluntarily, by forming separate sex-specific groups. Teachers already actively intervene to use girls as 'neutralizing elements' to counter male aggressiveness in group activities, so more collaborative work between girls and boys is possible, if teachers so decide.

The Use of Space

Boys have a very strong tendency to dominate spaces in general use, e.g. at breaks between classes or at playtimes. Girls are thus consigned to meet in corners or in lavatories, where they have to put up with constant harassment and aggression from boys.

Playgrounds in mixed schools tend to be planned according to boys' needs (and boys play football for the most part). This situation is common to most schools and hardly anyone seems aware of the need for change.

Attitude of Teachers

Most teachers seem to think that the problem of sex discrimination has been solved by making schools coeducational. Generally speaking, teachers are unaware of the nature of sexism and sex discrimination and are even less aware of their role as transmission agents. Therefore, they constantly (often unconsciously) reinforce sexist stereotypes through their own actions and teaching.

Aggression

The subordinated position of women in society has traditionally resulted in regular acts of violence and aggression which have been played down or dismissed. Women have struggled for the right to gain access to all fields of study and work including education. However, they have had to pay a price for their success and underground hostility has become more open.

So when girls entered coeducational centres (in our country later than in others) without asking for changes to essentially male institutions, they experienced the same forms of violence, the public silence over which marked the limits of their subordinate position. As soon as girls and women became more feminist in their demands, harassment became more explicit.

Thus girls who try to give up their submissive, passive and obedient roles are subject to constant physical and verbal aggression from their male peers who fear losing their privileged and superior position. (Something similar happens to women teachers and other women workers in the street and in the home.) The importance of this harassment towards girls tends to be minimized or considered as trivial by those teachers who feel this type of male/female behaviour to be 'natural'. They sometimes even encourage it!

Since the violent male model is encouraged in the school, serious problems arise about the possibilities of coexistence between the sexes in the classroom. Girls are frequently used as 'neutralizing agents' to counter the aggression of the boys, as has already been mentioned. Thus girls are handicapped in two further ways in the moves toward coeducation – they have lost their right to be taught separately from boys, and they have lost their right *not* to have direct contact with the aggressive behaviour of their male peers.

NON-INSTITUTIONAL ALTERNATIVES IN THE FIGHT AGAINST SEXISM IN EDUCATION

In the early 1970s, several women's groups within the feminist movement included in their demands the need to eliminate sexism from the education system. We include a list of women's groups currently dealing with this issue in the appendix to this chapter.

The main goals of these women's groups has been to collect data about the everyday realities of schooling and to analyse evidence on the extent of sexism within educational institutions.

As a consequence of this analysis, the reality of male/female relations has been discussed at staff meetings in order for the necessary changes to be made. In most cases, recommendations for change have not been well received by the education community, and it has been left to women teachers, either individually or in groups, to undertake anti-sexist activities.

At more progressive schools the need for change has now been recognized and, in theory, women teachers (and mothers) are now entitled to the same recognition and status as their male equivalents. Nevertheless, when put into practice, such changes have been strongly resisted and have received little backing. Indeed, there has been clear opposition to any changes that may affect the privileged male hierarchy.

Below we list some of the practical activities which have been tried out by women teachers:

- Drama activities including plays concerning the nature of sex-roles.
- Murals containing pictures of women and men doing the same activities.
- 'Books of Pictures' which similarly show women and men doing the same jobs and activities.
- Traditional tales, songs and poems with revised non-sexist wording, but conserving the original story-line and music.
- Creation of an alternative, non-sexist dictionary.
- At playtime, the promotion of mixed-sex games formerly considered exclusive to one sex or the other.
- Creating mixed-sex teams for sports with a view to establishing that competition should be concerned with

improving one's own performance rather than competing with others.

- Investigations about the images of women in the newspapers and media.
- Rotating turns in the allocation of tasks and responsibilities in the classroom (discipline, captain of the sports team, participation in assembly, etc.).
- Carrying out surveys on different topics. For instance, who does homework? Which are the most popular professions and careers among pupils? What do pupils feel about harassment? What are their most popular hobbies?
- Arranging debates on events which affect pupils or asking for their views about stereotypes.
- Focusing on women in history and women's contributions to literature, the arts and other cultural fields.

None of these activities can easily be carried out in educational institutions as they require a great deal of work and effort as well as highly qualified professionals who understand the sexist mechanisms of schooling.

INSTITUTIONAL POLICIES FOR THE PROMOTION OF EQUALITY OF OPPORTUNITY IN EDUCATION

The Institute of the Woman was founded in 1983. It is an administrative body with responsibility for the creation of policies for equality. In 1986, an agreement was signed between the Institute and the Ministry of Education, the latter committing itself to carry out a programme of teacher training concerned with promoting equality of opportunity.

The first training course was held in September 1987. Thirty-seven people attended, each of whom was responsible for the promotion of equal opportunities within a (different) teaching centre. Although the programme was enthusiastically received, it has proved totally inadequate in coping with the needs of teachers given that there are currently 160,000 teachers in the country's infant and primary schools. The speed of training is far too slow despite the fact that the programme is still in operation.

On the other hand, the initial training of teachers, still dependent on the universities, does not address the practical issues of sex discrimination, thus neglecting this aspect of teachers' work.

At the time of writing, the government has promised to mount the Plan of Equality of Opportunity for Women (1988–1990) which, in respect of education, means revisions to the Resolution of 3 June 1985, of the Council and the Ministers of Education of the European Community (EEC). So far, the goals set out within the framework of this Plan have not been enforced through development of policy by the Ministry of Education.

However, as a result of Spain's entry into the EEC, specific actions have been initiated besides the training programme for teaching staff. Action research aimed at stimulating the participation of girls in activities related to the New Information Technologies (NIT) is being carried out in two schools in the province of Madrid and a poster competition for girls and boys, for the design of non-sexist images, was held in 1987. The Ministry of Education has also sponsored innovatory projects in the field of coeducation and the Institute of the Woman currently funds women's groups dealing with anti-sexist issues. It also promotes research and produces publications.

SOME CONCLUSIONS

Feminists, in their struggles against the structures of patriarchy, have challenged the ideology and organization of an essentially androcentric and hierarchical education system, unsuitable for either sex to be taught in.

We are aware that education cannot be separated from society. On the contrary, we recognize that it transmits and strongly reinforces the dominant social principles and structures. Therefore, alternative proposals only make sense if they critically address the system itself. We thus demand:

- a critical analysis of the hierarchies of existing social systems which result in subordinate status for women;
- the adoption of non-androcentric perspectives, particularly in the sciences and at a practical level;
- encouragement to enable people to pursue needs and interests undetermined by sex stereotypes;
- modification of the language in order to create the possibilities of better forms of communication and knowledge;

This should be an alternative to the present role of language which, in providing barriers to women, as described earlier, perpetuates itself as an important power base for men;

- support for changes in ideas and models about interpersonal relationships;
- redefinition of the goals and institutional policies in terms of greater social equality and the provision of the necessary means to achieve them.

Bearing in mind that sex inequality is socially constructed and that education is part of that construction, we strongly defend the education system in the interests of girls and women and shall continue to do so until the principles of the patriarchal system no longer have a place in schooling or society.

APPENDIX

Below we list some women's groups at present dealing with these matters:

Colectivo de educación no sexista de Enseñanza Secundaria Madrid (Non-sexist Education Collective of Secondary Education)

Colectivo por una escuela infantil no sexista, Madrid (Collective for a non-sexist infant school)

Colectivo por una escuela no sexista, Oviedo (Collective for a non-sexist school)

Asamblea de dones denseyament, Barcelona

Colectivo Lamiarri, Pamplona (Lamiarri Collective)

Asamblea de dones, Mallorca

Colectivo Muyer y Educación, Canary Islands (Women and Education Collective)

Grupo Ostadar, Bilbao (Ostadar Group)

Feminario, Alicante

Asamblea de mujeres, Cantabria (Women's Assembly)

Asociación Feminista de Asturias, Asturias (Feminist Association of Asturias)

Frente Feminista, Saragossa (Feminist Front)

Asociación de Ingenieras y Architectas, Madrid (Women Engineers and Women Architects)

Asamblea de Mujers, Seville (Women's Assembly)

Colectivo Feminista 'A favor de las niñas', Madrid (Feminist Collective 'In favour of the girls')

CHAPTER 6

Scotland

Doris Dick

Scotland is a part of the United Kingdom, yet is independent in a number of contexts; one such context is education. This chapter seeks to explain the structure of Scottish education and how it has been influenced by the 1975 Sex Discrimination Act and other policy developments. It then considers how the Scottish primary school and teacher training institutions have, or have not, dealt with equal opportunities issues and finally speculates about possibilities for future progress.

THE SCOTTISH EDUCATION SYSTEM

Scotland, a country within the United Kingdom, is governed by British law and sends elected representatives to the British Parliament in London. In some respects, however, Scotland maintains a degree of independence: it has its own legal system and its own education system. In general, laws which are passed in London apply within Scotland, or are modified to accord with Scots law. Thus it was with the Sex Discrimination Act (1975) which, among other things, obliged education authorities in Scotland to offer all aspects of the school curriculum to all children.

However, what appeared on the surface to be a straightforward matter for schools and education authorities to implement has taken years to be made a reality, and in some instances the finer points of the Act are still being debated and only gradually absorbed into the ethos of the classroom. The exact effect of the Sex Discrimination Act on the Scottish primary school classroom is difficult to assess as no research has yet been done on this subject.

THE SEX DISCRIMINATION ACT (1975)

The Sex Discrimination Act, which applies to the whole of the United Kingdom, makes sex discrimination unlawful in education, training, employment, and similar areas. It gives individuals direct access to the civil courts and industrial tribunals, allowing them to take legal action against unlawful discrimination – for example, treating anyone on the grounds of gender less favourably than a person of the opposite sex would be treated in the same circumstances. In education, this means, among other things, that pupils should have access to education irrespective of sex.

In Scotland, as elsewhere in the United Kingdom, the education system is undergoing a series of changes, particularly in terms of its management structure. At the moment, schools in Scotland are run by education authorities which operate within each region. The directorate, which consists of nine regional and three island councils, has a total staff of 478, less than a fifth of whom are women.[1] Each education authority is responsible for all state primary and secondary schools in its region. At the head of each authority is a director of education.

There are no women directors of education, and most women education officers are advisers and curriculum development officers in subjects such as English, guidance and primary education. There are five assistant directors who are women. In all cases, men control finance and policy.

Each education authority, being responsible for policy within its region (and therefore for deciding how much emphasis should be given to particular issues), determines what requirements should be placed on schools to formulate policies of their own. Thus, the response to the Sex Discrimination Act has varied from region to region, and from school to school.

The Scottish Education Department, which is concerned with the overall management of the system, has four women officers, the highest of whom is at principal-officer level. The inspectorate inspects schools and higher education establishements, advises on policy and administration, and assists with curricular development. It has 12 women out of a total of 114, all at the most junior level of the hierarchy. The only significant improvement in the representation of women in management roles between 1979 and 1984 was in the number of women headteachers in primary schools. Around 89 per cent of primary school teachers are women; in 1979 around 50 per cent of headteachers were women, but by 1984 this had risen to 60 per cent.

Several years elapsed after the passing of the Act before any policy document[2] was issued to schools by an education authority in Scotland. Even then, the document issued by Lothian Region to its schools merely outlined the letter of the law making no attempt to develop what might be called 'the spirit of the Act'. In fact, in many Lothian schools the document was never seen by class teachers. It was received by the headteachers and acted on or filed away as they saw fit. The region is, however, presently considering re-issuing the document to teachers as a way of ensuring that they are aware of its contents. It is only recently that Strathclyde, the largest authority in Scotland, has required equal opportunities statements to be included in school prospectuses. Inaction on the part of education authorities has allowed discriminatory practices to continue in Scottish schools for many years after they should, in theory, have been outlawed.

SCHOOLS' COUNCILS

Schools' Councils are panels which meet regularly to discuss matters of educational interest at a local level. They are made up of head teachers and staff representatives from the local secondary school and its feeder primary schools, elected parent representatives from all schools involved, local councillors, a member of the church, and secondary school pupils. In the past, such bodies have been involved in policy making, and it is surprising that they have not been more enthusiastic about promoting equal opportunities. However, it seems as if the Schools' Councils will soon be abolished, to be replaced by groups with greater emphasis on parent participation. It remains to be seen whether these new bodies will press any more effectively for the implementation of a sound equal opportunities policy.

PROGRESS IN THE PRIMARY SCHOOLS

In Scotland, children begin school at about the age of five. They remain in full-time education until they are sixteen – eleven years of compulsory full-time education, seven of which are spent in the primary school. The years in the primary school are those when the child is particularly impressionable, when the messages received about the nature of the world and the roles of the people in it may prove especially influential in the child's development.

For most primary teachers, the provision of equal access to the curriculum has meant teaching the boys sewing and the girls craft or woodwork. Few realize that the problem is more complex than this and requires a complete reappraisal of teaching methods and content. In general, it has been left to the individual teachers and headteachers to deal with the matter in their own classrooms and schools. The main difficulty is that without any guidance from management, or focused debate within the system at large, they may not even see the need to promote equal opportunities. In fact, many do not perceive that the problem actually exists.

Differences between the sexes in terms of subject choice at secondary school have been fairly well documented, but the crucial role of the primary school in helping children to develop a positive self-image has received less attention. At this important stage, the child at school is quite likely to be surrounded by male imagery in visual material, in reading schemes, in factual course work which focuses on men's achievements, and by the dominance of football in the playground. Without effort and sensitivity on the part of the primary teacher, women and their achievements may remain invisible. By the time they reach secondary school boys tend to have been bombarded by positive images of men on whom to base their expectations. Girls on the other hand are often asked to make their career choices in a vacuum.

SCHOOL CURRICULUM

In the vast majority of Scottish schools, the pupil register lists the children in alphabetical order, with boys first, and children are often required to move into and around the school building in separate lines of girls and boys. In some instances, boys and girls may be taught physical education in single-sex groups, and, in one school at least, the boys enjoy football training whilst the girls are given extra geography – colouring in maps. In the same school, one eleven-year-old boy expressed his sympathy for the girls when rehearsing for the school's production of *Chariots of Fire* – 'There are no parts in it for the girls, just ones where they make tea.'

The importance of raising teacher awareness of the issues involved in promoting equal opportunities in the primary school is paramount. At a time of ever-decreasing spending in education, teachers may fall back more on texts which portray increasingly outdated stereotypes. Or alternatively, when creating their own resources, they may reproduce similar stereotypes themselves.

Occasionally, parents have been the ones to bring such sexist stereotyping to the teacher's attention, as happened in one school recently. A teacher asked her class of eight-year-olds to complete a list showing what a mother does, what a father does and what the child does. Examples were supplied in the book:

A Mother	A Father	Myself
she washes	he travels	I learn
she cleans	he works	I play

One parent out of the class of twenty-eight complained about the sexist nature of the examples contained in this piece of work. The teacher herself had not realized that the work was sexist or that it might be offensive, and even after it was brought to her attention, argued that the child could have entered any action as being appropriate to a mother or father. However, the prescriptive nature of the examples and their stereotyped nature was borne out in the way that another child completed the the exercise:

she polishes	he drives	I work
she dries	he mends	I skip
she hoovers	he snoozes	I sleep

The correct usage of verbs would seem to be only one of the lessons to be learned here. Teachers can, however, be resistant to having their view of the world challenged. In discussing the above example, another teacher commented, 'But that is what happens, that is how the world is. Why shouldn't you use that example? It seems fair enough to me.'

TEACHER TRAINING AND IN-SERVICE TRAINING

Such comments and examples constitute a strong argument in favour of in-service teacher training. Working teachers should be provided with courses which deal directly with the question of equality in the classroom. And these should be supplied by local educational advisory services, and other groups, to ensure that innovations in education theory and practice do not go unnoticed.

Those of us in Scotland who are concerned about equal opportunities see this as a matter of utmost urgency. Edinburgh Women in Education, a pressure group of teachers and parents concerned with the promotion of equal opportunities in Lothian schools, has been working with the Regional Women's Committee to find ways of making equality a high profile issue in the region. Together they are pressing Lothian Region Education Department to designate equal opportunities as a future mainstream in-service topic.

Schools would then be encouraged to discuss and debate the Regional guidelines and create for themselves a school policy which would outline how to develop good and positive practice. Specialist speakers might be brought in both to highlight how classroom resources presenting women more positively can be created, and to encourage teachers to be more aware of the negative imagery to be found in some, often older, texts.

While Lothian Region is deciding whether or not to focus on equality as an in-service issue, the picture elsewhere in Scotland tends to be equally uncertain. However, there are examples of positive action to be found, which I suggest hold the seeds of future progress.

KINNEIL PRIMARY

One such example is that of Kinneil Primary School in Central Region. Margaret Connarty has been headteacher there for the last eight years and in that time has piloted the adoption of an equal opportunities policy by her staff. It was Margaret Connarty's own interest and involvement in equal opportunities which raised the profile of the subject within the school. At Kinneil, a whole school policy was developed in consultation with the school staff.

That original policy is currently being updated as part of a comprehensive policy covering race, sex, and learning difficulties. Parents have been involved in the discussions since the beginning, and at all stages of development. Each member of staff, including catering staff and janitors, is required to address the question of equality, enabling it to be employed evenly throughout the school.

An interventionist approach has been adopted by the teaching staff, based on the rule that children must work and co-operate in mixed-sex groups in all school activities. In this way, children can come to understand and appreciate each other as individuals.

School activities are seen as extending beyond the classroom and the direct control of the teacher, into playground games at break and lunchtime. Here too, school policy decrees that groups and teams should be mixed. In a situation where one sex is dominating an area, or a piece of equipment, teacher intervention is essential in order to redress the balance. Positive encouragement is given to girls to play with Lego, an area in which the boys had dominated in the infant classes. Again, when travelling around the school, the children move in mixed groups. Teachers are alerted to the need for positive images of women around the school and for careful vetting of books and other learning materials for sex bias.

THE FUTURE IN SCOTLAND

At the time of writing, and on the evidence of the past fifteen years, change is very slow in coming. There is evidence that the problem is being taken more seriously but mainly in response to pressure from concerned, and often isolated, groups of teachers and parents. One place where innovation and progress should surely be sought is within the teacher training colleges. If tomorrow's primary teachers are to be aware of the issues involved in providing equal opportunities in their classrooms, the colleges should be tackling the problem with them. They should be promoting research, helping with the preparation of unbiased resources, and investigating classroom management techniques aimed at achieving an equal distribution of teacher time.

The colleges should give some lead to future teachers. At present Moray House College of Education in Edinburgh has no policy statement on equal opportunities. The issue at Moray House, one of Scotland's major training colleges, remains a matter of internal debate, although it is hoped that it will soon be incorporated in a policy document. In the meantime, students there are given the general advice to be aware of racism and sexism when preparing worksheets; but they receive few practical guidelines and are, by and large, forced to rely on their own levels of awareness. When Scotland's colleges succeed in raising these levels of awareness its primary schools will start to benefit.

NOTES

1 *The Education Authorities Directory and Annual*, 1987.

2 Lothian Region Education Committee: *Equal Opportunities: Guidelines for Schools, Colleges and Community Education*. Lothian Region has provided training for all personnel involved in selction procedures in order to prevent discrimination. This programme is due to reach completion in the near future.

CHAPTER 7

Ireland

Lila Blount

INTRODUCTION

The Irish Sex Discrimination Act of 1977 provided the legislative framework for greater equality by establishing the Employment Equality Agency (EAA), which was to work within education as well as in other fields. For over a decade, therefore, there has been a commitment by the Irish government to promoting equal opportunities in education. This chapter considers some of the events and activities that have helped to further the cause of sex equality in Irish education and also charts some of the structural problems and obstacles to achieving that objective.

The following events are currently taking place in Ireland. Progress is very slow and sometimes obscure. We are, at the time of writing, in the midst of a serious recession, so that developments appear to be at a standstill. Perhaps it is to be expected in this situation, but it is certainly not acceptable. Equality is the very kernel of a good education system. For centuries, the system has been biased and it urgently needs serious revision and change. For those who have a burning desire to see justice being done in all areas, it has been a frustrating time. To grow an oak, a tiny seed has to be planted. It is to be hoped that one day equality will be likened to the oak, spreading out in all directions with roots extending and firmly planted.

GOVERNMENT INITIATIVES IN EQUAL OPPORTUNITIES IN EDUCATION

In 1984, the then Irish Minister for Education, Gemma Hussey, decided to make the theme 'Equality of Opportunity for Girls' one of the major issues for attention during the Irish Presidency of the Education Committee of the European Communities. By doing this she ensured that the topic, which had previously received only erratic attention from that committee, would become part of the Community's long-term action plan in education. The success of this initiative can be judged by two events. The first was a major conference on Equality of Opportunity in Education held in Brussels in November 1984. This conference brought together, for the first time, educational personnel, personnel from equal opportunity agencies, politicians and parents from all ten EEC countries. All worked together to draw up recommendations both for a European Community Policy and for use in each of the ten countries represented at the meeting.

The second event, which followed from the above, was the decision by the Ministers for Education of the European Community, of which Ireland is a member, to adopt, on 3 June 1985, a Council Resolution containing an action programme on equal opportunities for girls and boys in education. By doing this, the Ministers pledged support for a programme of action which promotes the principle of equal opportunity in education at all levels as well as meeting the needs which were identified the previous November in Brussels. The resolution also signified agreement to use funds for this purpose from the Commission's budget as well as from member countries' education budgets.

The Ministers were agreed that special measures were necessary in order to ensure equal access to education and training, to enable appropriate educational and career choices to be made, to motivate students to make non-traditional choices and to encourage girls to participate in the new and expanding sectors in education and training. The first initiative, taken by the European Commission under the Action Programme, has been the publication of the Action Handbook *How to Implement Gender Equality*. The Commission has also set up a working group with representatives from all the EEC countries to decide upon other cross-Europe activities which might promote equality of opportunity in education and to facilitate the exchange of experience and information on successful projects. The Commission has also given a new thrust to the equality issue under the EEC scheme of 'Study Visits for Educationalists' in member states by ensuring that every year a group from each country will have as the theme of the study visit 'Equality of Opportunity in Education'.

IRISH NATIONAL TEACHERS' INITIATIVES ON EQUAL OPPORTUNITIES IN PRIMARY EDUCATION

In 1981, a study entitled 'Equality of Opportunity in Primary School Teaching' in Ireland was undertaken by the Educational Research Centre (ERC), following a joint initiative on the part of the Irish National Teachers' Organization (INTO) and the Employment Equality Agency (EEA). The purpose of the meeting was to consider steps which might be taken to promote equal opportunity in primary- (national-) school teaching. A steering committee, with representatives from these organizations and from other teacher unions and from the Department of Education was formed, to advise on the execution of the study and to monitor its progress.

The broad objectives of the study were to:

(a) Examine the factors which lead to success in securing appointment and promotion in primary school teaching and assess whether these factors differ for men and women;
(b) Examine the factors which influence teachers to seek promotion and to determine whether they differ for men and women;
(c) Establish the attitudes of men and women towards equality of opportunity in primary teaching.

Two major sources of data were used in the study. Information from Department of Education and INTO files provided general statistics on the population of teachers. The second source was the responses of a sample of teachers to a questionnaire which had been sent out in March 1982. The distribution of the questionnaire was confined to the members of INTO, and 1,438 (71.9 per cent) of the original 2,000 sent were completed and returned. The final report was published in June 1986 under the title *Gender Inequalities in Primary School Teaching* and its findings are detailed in the next section. As far as I know, at the time of writing, this has been the only major study on equal opportunities in Ireland.

INEQUALITIES IN TEACHER APPOINTMENTS TO PROMOTED POSTS: THE REPORT

A number of interesting findings emerged from this study.

Almost three-quarters (72.9 per cent) of INTO members were women, indicating that the overall ratio proportion of women to men was 2.69 : 1. (In the total population of teachers, including non-INTO members, 74.0 per cent were women, giving a ratio of 2.85 : 1.) These ratios were not maintained at promotional levels, however. Among INTO members the percentage of women who were principals (heads) was only 7.8 per cent (or 10.5 per cent if privileged assistants[1] were included), while the percentage of men was 38.7 (or 40.3 per cent if privileged assistants were included). Thus, a male primary teacher was almost five times more likely to become a principal than his female colleague (4.96 : 1), or just under four times as likely if privileged assistants are included (3.84 : 1). The position of women was slightly better for the post of teaching principal[2] than it was for principalships in general; 33.7 per cent of men held the post of teaching principal as against 7.0 per cent of women. Women's position in larger schools was worse. Five per cent of men were principals in large schools (walking principals[2]), whereas only 0.8 per cent of women were.

Women were more likely to hold the post of privileged assistant (1.69 times more likely) than men. In fact, the vast majority (81.9 per cent) of privileged assistants were women. This suggests that in school amalgamations, men have been fairly consistently appointed to the position of principal. Men have also had an advantage in Grade A and Grade B posts. The proportion of men to women in grade A posts was 1.4 : 1, the proportion in grade B posts 1.04 : 1. Women, on the other hand, were much more likely to be vice-principals[3] (1 : 1.57) and, of course, to be assistant teachers (1 : 1.64).

[1]Privileged Assistants are those teachers who have amalgamated with another school and have lost the title Principal but retained their increments and are called Privileged Assistants.
[2]Teaching Principal. A principal or head of school who teaches a class because the school is small and has fewer than eight teachers. Eight teachers constitute a 'walking principal'. This is a principal who does not teach (a class).
[3]Vice-Principalship is a seniority post which teachers obtain automatically.

The basic facts about sex differences in promoted posts in the primary school teaching service are unambiguous. Women are seriously under-represented in such posts. The situation is not one that has arisen overnight, but certainly seems to have worsened over time. Women appear to be at a disadvantage in all types of school. However, the degree of disadvantage varies somewhat between school types. Their position relative to men is worse in lay, rural, all-grade schools. A teacher's experience in teaching senior classes in primary school has traditionally been related to promotion, and, in the main, women's experience of such classes is more limited than that of their male colleagues. If matters are to be improved, either the status of such classes should be revised or women should be given greater opportunities to teach at a more senior level. While, in general, women reported having taught in a wider range of grades than had men, their experiences were more likely to have been in junior than in senior grades. It would appear that teaching experience in lower grades does not count for much in the promotion stakes.

Although the teachers in the sample clearly felt that sex and marital status should not be factors in determining whether or not one was appointed to a post of assistant teacher or to a post of principal, they recognized that this was not what happened in reality. Some teachers reported overt discrimination in the appointments procedure.

On 1 January 1985, the Department of Education adopted INTO proposals for amendment of the rules governing appointment of principal and assistant teachers in order to promote equality of opportunity and to eliminate discrimination. The revised rules impose a series of obligations on school management bodies, including the following:

- each post shall be advertised nationally;
- applications shall be invited from eligible men and women teachers;
- each selection board shall include at least one man and one woman;
- the selection board shall establish criteria for shortlisting and assessment of candidates;
- the chairperson of the selection board shall keep records of these criteria and of the interviews;

- the selection shall have regard to equality legislation and shall not ask discriminatory questions;
- all questions shall relate to the requirements of the post.

SEXISM IN PRIMARY EDUCATION

The concept of curriculum for national schools can be interpreted more broadly than just as a set of subjects with specific content. In this section, then, I shall refer to both the formal and the 'hidden' curriculum. The *hidden* curriculum is the name given to that which pupils learn in schools which is not deliberately taught as part of the official curriculum, (e.g. disciplinary procedures, staffing arrangements, teaching materials, teacher attitudes, etc.).

The official curriculum for national schools is contained in two handbooks published by the Department of Education, the first in 1971. All subjects specified in the curriculum are compulsory for both boys and girls. The introduction to the curriculum states that:

> The aim of primary education is to enable the child to live a full life as a child and to equip him [sic] to avail himself of further education so that he may go on to live a full and useful life as an adult in society.

A close examination of the curriculum reveals sex-stereotyping in the treatment of boys and girls in certain subjects, in particular, music and PE. An extract from the music curriculum states that:

> Some songs are particularly suited to boys e.g. martial, gay, humorous, rhythmic airs. Others are more suited to girls e.g. lullabies, spinning songs, songs tender in content and expression.

This is a clear reinforcement of the image of men as assertive, humorous and intelligent, compared to women, who are depicted as soft, passive, gentle and dependent. The implementation of this part of the recommended programme in music denies both boys and girls a whole range of experiences and skills in one of the most vital arts. A similar segregation of girls and boys is proposed in parts of the PE syllabus. It suggests that separate arrangements in movement training be made for boys and girls.

Boys can now acquire a wide variety of skills and techniques and girls often become aware of style and grace.

Children absorb what they see and feel. They see men more likely to be in positions of power and authority. They see men doing a greater variety of jobs, yet it is the women, their mothers, who play the major role in caring for and supporting them. In school language programmes, when children are asked 'Do Mammy and Daddy work?', their replies are inevitably indicative of how they perceive the Mammy/Daddy roles: 'Yes, Daddy works but Mammy does not.' Mammy is taken for granted and housework is not considered to be 'work'. These attitudes are further encouraged by the primary textbooks. Their observations of reality show the books to be deeply sexist, yet in order for the books to change, reality has also to change. Teachers should, nevertheless, try to ensure that what is presented to children in school through their interactions with the teachers, through teacher attitudes and classroom materials, does not reinforce outdated, stereotyped roles.

As well as learning from the behaviour and attitudes of their teachers, children also learn about sex roles from their textbooks, as has already been indicated. School books are presented within a context of authority – the classroom. This context conveys official approval for attitudes children will have learned at home, from television and from other social experiences. In the Irish schooling system at present, textbooks are the main instrument by which children become literate. Gemma Hussey, when Minister for Education, recognized this when she met the Irish educational publishers in 1984 to discuss sexism and sex-stereotyping in textbooks. She argued that many pupils have total faith in what their textbooks tell them, and she issued the *International Reading Association Guidelines* to enable the publishers to evaluate better sex-stereotyping in reading material. When using these guidelines, we see that many of the books being used in Irish schools at present portray an inaccurate view of the world. Many women, nowadays, either through choice or necessity, work outside the home but as one author wrote, 'the apron syndrome' is all too common in our textbooks (NATE, 1985). In many books, the only female characters working outside the homes are teachers, freelance witches and the occasional cook.

The Rainbow Reading Scheme is widely used in Irish schools

and is an English language reading scheme. The early books in the scheme show Mammy driving the car and Anne playing with a lorry, but that seems to mark the limits of their attempt at non-sex-stereotyping. By the time we come to the next book *Fun on the Farm*, for senior infants, we see Uncle Jack and Barry washing the tractor and Aunt Mary and Anne looking on. The passive role of women is all too common in our textbooks. *Treasure Seeker* and *Crock of Gold*, books for the fifth and sixth classes, each contained only four stories where women are the main characters. One story portrays a woman in a particularly denigrating way – the nagging wife of Walter Mitty.

Irish language books are similarly stereotyped. One book has a story about the Bishop coming to visit the school and Niamh wanting a new dress for the occasion. Mammy, Daddy, Niamh and Pol (Paul, Niamh's brother) go shopping. Niamh selects her outfit but comments to Mammy that it is very expensive. Mammy agrees but says that Daddy has plenty of money. She calls on Daddy to pay and he says 'You have me broke', at which Pol intervenes to say that his clothes are good enough for the occasion and declares 'Aren't women very expensive, Daddy?' At best, this story teaches a necessary tolerance of the 'tiresome and expensive ways' of women, at worst it teaches contempt!

In the area of maths, everyday problems that can be viewed mathematically seem to revolve around the world of football, men driving cars, trains and buses and male earning power and property ownership. This occours with all topics, whether statistics, measurement or velocity. The world of maths is male and this is reinforced in several books by the number of questions depicting men and boys doing things susceptible to mathematical calculations. The only references to female ownership or earning power are placed in a sexist context. For example, the following problem is posed in a fourth-year textbook: 'A woman had 104 hens, 1/4 of them were white and the rest were brown. How many were white?', whilst men earned, left wills, owned land, etc. (*Busy at Maths*, Book four).

The fact that the majority of school textbooks are written and edited by males must account, in part, for the biased view of male and female roles, which in turn influences the minds and views of the children who read them.

The administration and management of national schools also

reinforces sex-stereotyping for children, as the survey on promotion and the primary teacher suggests. Departmental inspectors, figures of authority, are most likely to be male. There are ninety inspectors serving primary schools in Ireland, and of these only *six* are women, five of whom were recruited in recent years. The majority of non-teaching principals of national schools, as I have already shown, are men, as are the all-important school caretakers. The chair of the school Board of Management is almost always a man! On the other hand, secretaries, cleaners, nurses and infant teachers are almost always women.

INTO LEGAL INITIATIVES: SOME SUCCESSES

At the time of writing, the INTO has had a very successful year (1987) in fighting discrimination against women teachers. Two boards of management have been found guilty of discrimination and decisions have been made in favour of three women teachers who had applied for principalships.

The largest award recommended under the 1977 anti-discrimination legislation was made in the case of a teacher in a primary school. The case was brought by INTO on behalf of a female teacher whose application for the principalship of a school in June 1986 was unsuccessful. INTO supported the teacher's claim that she had been treated less favourably at the interview because she was a woman. After a full investigation of all the criteria used in making the appointment, the Equality Officer of the Labour Court found in favour of the female teacher and recommended that she should be paid £11,000 in compensation by the Board of Management of the school (INTO Annual Report at Annual Congress (1988)).

In the other case, two women teachers who had applied for the principalship of a large junior school alleged that they had been discriminated against on the grounds of sex and marital status. Both were awarded £300 on the recommendation of the equality officer of the Labour Court. One of the women alleged that the questions asked of her concerning her family responsibilities constituted discrimination under the terms of the Employment Equality Act. The equality officer found that the questions asked at interview placed an onus on the applicant to show that her family responsibilities would not interfere with her ability to undertake and perform the work of a principal. It was clear that male and female applicants were not asked similar questions regarding their family responsibilities. In the case of the other complainant, the equality officer found that two members of the selection board had discriminated against her on the basis of her sex and had failed to justify the low marks they had awarded her (INTO Annual Report, Annual Congress 1987/88.)

These cases have provided a major boost for the promotion of equality of opportunity in primary teaching. Women teachers will, in future, have more confidence in applying for promotions, knowing that their applications must be treated fairly, and that, where discrimination does take place, it can be challenged. It will also, it is hoped, prove a strong reminder to boards of management, which are responsible for the appointment of teachers.

TEACHERS TO PROMOTE GENDER EQUALITY IN EDUCATION (TPGEE); AN INFORMAL OUT-OF-SCHOOL EQUAL OPPORTUNITIES INITIATIVE

Smaller, voluntary groupings have also a place in the struggle for greater equality. Following a conference organized by a group of teachers to raise awareness of inequalities in the Irish education system, TPGEE was formed in September 1985, with the aim of improving equality in education and pushing for change in teachers' attitudes, especially in primary schools. All issues were to be addressed, from promotion of female staff to sexist literature. The membership of this group has been exclusively female even though it is open to all teachers. It has also comprised mainly primary school teachers. Development of the group has been slow, principally because it has been largely self-financing, with only a small contribution from a teachers' centre, to buy resource books on sexism.

This group, nevertheless, organized the first in-service course for teachers on 'Gender in the Primary School System', comprising a series of lectures which examined the way language reproduces and reinforces gender distinctions, the development of gender identity in early childhood, women in trade unions, women's involvement in history, and the 'fear to confront', i.e. the problem of feminine assertion. Teachers who attended were very generous in their praise of the course.

The TPGEE, as a voluntary group, is not able to find the

time to make contact with official education bodies or other groups, though it would like more assistance and backing from educational authorities. The group is, however, affiliated to, and receives help from, the Women's Studies Association of Ireland. TPGEE has criticized the lack of government interest in equality issues, noting that the only time equality formed part of national education policy was during 1983–4, when the Minister for Education was a woman and was interested in equality. However, despite these efforts, the school inspectorate remains indifferent. An example given by the group was an inspectors' conference in 1984, at which equality was number 37 of issues up for discussion and coincidentally the last item on the list of priorities in drawing up a school plan. However, TPGEE continues to meet and hopes to undertake some research in the near future. One member is currently interviewing and writing short stories on famous women in Ireland. It is hoped to publish these monthly in school magazines from September 1988.

WOMEN'S STUDIES ASSOCIATION OF IRELAND (WSAI)

Another equality venture in education has been that of the Women's Studies Association of Ireland. WSAI was founded in June 1984, with membership open to anyone interested in the development of women's studies in Ireland. Teaching and research staff in third-level (tertiary) institutions, including universities, teacher-education colleges, regional technical colleges, secondary and primary schools were all strongly represented. In April 1985, WSAI made a submission to the Curriculum and Examinations Board (CEB) entitled 'Towards a New Curriculum: Gender and Schooling'. The issues that arise in the interaction of gender with education are basic issues for the association. In their own studies, many of its members have experienced particular problems connected with gender inequalities in the Irish education system. Many members have followed the growing body of feminist research, criticism and theory on gender and education in Ireland and in the UK. The association itself constitutes a resource that is available to assist both the CEB and the Department of Education in the formulation and implementation of policies designed to eliminate sexism in education.

102

The contribution of women's studies has not been confined to the education of girls and women. It is seen as equally essential for the education of boys and men so that, for example, they can appreciate the achievements of women. It also follows that women's studies should not be regarded as an 'extra option', however desirable, tacked on to the established mainstream curriculum. Women's studies should be valued as an integral component of mainstream human studies. It is also a 'strategy for change' where the existing curriculum is clearly inadequate and promotes unacceptable gender socialization. Women's studies can provide both the tools and the methods for 'radical' action.

WSAI has realized that change cannot be accomplished overnight where both the overt and hidden curricula are involved. The incorporation of feminist perspectives, knowledge and theory into the accepted mainstream of educational thought will be a long process. Change in the hidden curriculum will be a difficult task. School managers, teachers and parents themselves have been socialized in a patriarchal society and have to learn to recognize patriarchal knowledge, behaviour and attitudes and how to deal with them. They have to be taught to become vigilant and aware of the extent to which they themselves transmit patriarchal values and sex-role stereotypes.

The WSAI also made recommendations to the CEB which strictly lay outside the terms of reference of the committee, but were necessary in order to set discussion in a wider context. These included:

1. Structures and decision-making:

   The education system has developed within a patriarchal society and its own organisation reflects the paradigm of male authority and female subordination and servicing. This situation constitutes inequity in itself and also places decision-making under patriarchal control. Defining and removing this inequity will not in itself necessarily create a more human education but it is an essential prerequisite for this. The present structure perpetuates the provision of patriarchal role-models for girls and boys and makes the incorporation of women's studies in the curriculum virtually impossible.

2. Teacher Education:

  Issues of gender and education cannot be successfully confronted within each level of the system in isolation. The knowledge and theory that is taught at third level provides the paradigm within which new knowledge and theory is generated. The knowledge and theory generated and then approved and validated at third level passes into the textbooks used in schools. Teachers at first and second levels are trained and moulded in third level institutions. Teacher education therefore forms another section of the submission.

Primary education is one of the most vital areas where gender equality in society can be promoted. We must approach the problem of inequality as near to its roots as possible. The home is where sex-stereotyping begins. Thus, parent education is of vital importance. This is an area which must be addressed if changes are to be made. In the meantime, education in sex equality must begin as soon as the child starts school. In order to do this, teachers need to be made aware of the issues, and school principals should have a definite policy on equality in their school plans. Going a step further, there should be 'a person' from the Department of Education to act as monitor and ensure that this policy is carried out in all schools.

In so small a country as Ireland, all this should be perfectly feasible. However, we are again in the midst of a recession, with all that implies. There are many teachers who continue to fight for equality, and it is to be hoped that eventually 'the fight' will be recognized, as not only a means to improve the lives of girls and women but perhaps as a preventative measure and cure for many of the general ills and problems of contemporary Irish society.

To educate we must change, to change we must educate.

BIBLIOGRAPHY

Gender Inequalities in Primary School Teaching, The Educational Company, Drumcondra. (A joint study by the Irish National Teachers' Organization, the Employment Equality Agency and the Educational Research Centre, Drumcondra.)

Government's Programme for Action in Education (1984–87), Dublin: Dept of Education.

Guidelines for Publishers on Sexism and Sex-Stereotyping in Primary School Textbooks, Dublin: Dept of Education.

Hyland, A. (1988) 'The Multi-Denominational Experience in the National School System in Ireland.' Paper submitted at the Annual Conference of the Educational Studies Association of Ireland.

INTO Annual Report (1987/88).

Ladden, M. (1987) 'Sexism in Textbooks.' Paper delivered at Feminism II Conference, Dublin.

Smith, A. *Breaking the Circle: The Position of Women Academics in Third-level Education in Ireland*, EEC Action Programme.

Submission to the Curriculum and Examinations Board from the Women's Studies Association of Ireland. 'Towards a New Curriculum: Gender & Schooling', April 1985.

Teachers Centre (1985) *Teachers to Promote Gender Equality in Education*, Dublin.

CHAPTER 8

Federal Republic of Germany

Rixa Borns

INTRODUCTION

In this chapter, I shall focus in particular on North-Rhine-Westphalia (NRW), the Land with the highest population in the Federal Republic of Germany. It is extremely difficult to provide a general view of the country as a whole, owing to its federal nature. Even though the analysis will be partial, I shall attempt to provide an insight into the specific problems and perspectives of working towards sex equity in West German primary schools. I write from the perspective of a primary teacher in NRW who has been for many years deeply committed to improving education in this Land.

Strictly speaking, there is no homogeneous primary school in the Federal Republic of Germany. Because of the political structure of the country, the eleven federal districts each assume jurisdiction over education policy. Even though there is some collaboration between Lands, primary school guidelines and the corresponding organizational forms differ and are, moreover, subject to changes at the instigation of political majorities.

THE PRIMARY SCHOOL IN NORTH-RHINE–WESTPHALIA (NRW)

Structure

In NRW primary school is compulsory for children aged 6 through 10. All schools are coeducational and all curricular subjects including needlework, sports and crafts are taught in mixed groups. According to constitutional law, schools must have a Christian orientation, though they are often denominational in character. In principle – with a few exceptions – they are state schools. About 75 per cent of primary teachers are women, 50 per cent of whom work part time. Only about 25 per cent of primary schools have a female headteacher.

Curriculum

In 1973, for the first time, curricula were specified for the primary schools in NRW (NRW Ministry of Education, 1973) which made all primary schools responsible for dealing with the problem of sex-role stereotyping in subject-matter. As no appropriate or recommended educational material had been placed at the teachers' disposal, the teachers themselves were at liberty to deal with this subject as they pleased – intensively or not. The outcome of this first initiative of the Ministry of Education – or rather of the resulting activities at the primary-school level – has never been evaluated.

Only when discussion about equal rights for women were brought more urgently to the political stage in the early 1980s, were there obvious consequences for the educational environment. Then the authors of school books began to change their texts. Nowadays, it is hard to find conventional role pattern clichés in the language and reading books of the primary school. There are also increasingly more stories about girls who behave in atypical ways. It is left to the arithmetic books to show mother still going shopping, while father is repairing the car.

These evident trends have perhaps persuaded the authors of the *Guidelines and Curricula for the Primary School* in NRW 1985 (NRW Ministry of Education, 1985) that there was no need to include the subject of sex equality – despite the fact that, in the same year, a separate special decree was issued by the Minister of Education referring to the 'consideration of specific women's concerns in the guidelines and curricula of the schools in NRW' (NRW Ministry of Education, 1985). The main principles of this circular are as follows:

At the preparation, subsequent development and revision of guidelines and curricula it should be recognized that:

- self-development, with maintenance of social responsibility, shall be equally attainable for girls and boys;

- a thematic analysis should be made of the specific living conditions of girls and women, in order to achieve a well-balanced representation of the importance of women and men in society;
- the interests of girls should be intentionally addressed and promoted in subject-matter relating to natural science and technical knowledge;
- it should be made explicit in the formulation of guidelines and curricula that female and male pupils should be involved equally.

Though this decree thus set out clear-cut themes, it had only a modest response, from the schools at least. Anyway, for the primary schools, it came too late. Since the decree and the guidelines for primary schools had been issued in the same year (1985), the later decree had little influence on the guidelines.

In general, there is currently little awareness of the decree in schools. On the other hand, many activities relating to educational policy on equal opportunities have been influenced by this decree. For example, the guidelines currently being prepared for secondary schools are obliged to take note of this decree. Research projects on girls are being carried out and school books are licensed only on the understanding that they advocate coeducation and are instrumental in eliminating, albeit gradually, biases related to female role patterns.

THE SITUATION OF GIRLS

Already in primary schools girls achieve at higher levels than boys. In general, girls are more highly motivated, more conscientious and more attentive, though both male and female teachers pay less attention to them (Schümer, 1985). Thus, the greater attention and encouragement that boys receive is not entirely to do with their more demanding behaviour — teachers discriminate as well.

Curriculum content also favours boys. Research has indicated that girls and boys hold different attitudes and make different choices. Girls are in general more interested and competent in person-related activities, whereas boys prefer more factual topics.

To achieve a balanced education for both girls and boys, there have to be changes in approaches to school subjects and experiences. Thus subject content should clearly refer to real-life situations, and activities should be based on them, enabling pupils to identify with the issues. Such changes, however, are blocked by a lack of awareness among teachers (both male and female). In general, subject content still continues to identify with the interests of boys, who are regarded as 'more important'. Not infrequently, teachers look after the interests of the boys in order to avoid aggressive behaviour and indiscipline.

Another factor of primary school life which is important for girls is the daily violence they undergo from boys. Harassment, hounding, boxing and other forms of physical and psychic aggression are commonly experienced. Here sex-specific dominant and subordinate attitudes and behaviours emerge and are acted out.

The causes of this situation are many and, without a doubt, only partially conditioned by the school and learning environment. Nevertheless, schools should respond to these challenges. They need to investigate causes that lie outside the school environment, particularly exploring the social and cultural implications of sex inequality.

Coeducation alone will not solve the problems of sex inequality but must be conceived as a pedagogic challenge. Only learning processes for girls and boys which are co-operative, open and undifferentiated, will aid progress towards equal opportunities. Even though some recent studies suggest that it may – in special cases – be better for girls to be taught in separate single-sex groups, this cannot justify the feminist suggestion of separate schooling for girls as a principle.

Many problems which appear at the micro-level of the classroom cannot be faced and solved in isolation at this level. Pupils are conditioned by the – often widely varying – socio-cultural patterns of their families as well as by the cultural and economic framework of society. Thus, fundamental changes to the school environment are closely linked to changes at the macro-level of society.

PROSPECTS

During the women's movement of the 1980s, women teachers established joint initiatives at regional level (e.g. women's union groups and the working group 'Frauen und Schule' [women and school] and in several cities, other different women's and feminist initiatives) in order to push for much-needed reforms. They used meetings, public relations, individual research studies and regular publications to develop awareness about prevailing attitudes, values and prejudices and to draw attention to situations which provide obstacles to equality.

Meanwhile, lesson plans and classroom materials addressing various aspects of equal opportunities have been created. Certainly there is still a distinct gap between existing theoretical approaches and the practical changes needed to increase equality. Scientific studies continue to confirm the disadvantageous position of girls, but also fail in their attempts to show how changes can be made to the practical learning models and processes in the primary school. Moreover, there is a lack of adequate teaching materials and insufficient in-service training programmes. Nevertheless, positive steps have been taken more recently.

Wider discussion on the general political context of women's advancement, e.g. discussing the value of quota systems in favour of women, has – directly and indirectly – affected questions about sex equity in schooling. But schooling, above all the primary school, is only able to support equality issues if female colleagues, at the very least, are committed to change. Many women teachers in the primary school conform to traditional sex-role patterns. So, for instance, many only work part time in the school in order to have more time for children and housework. Thus, they themselves are living by principles which could be properly questioned in the learning context. Equal opportunities for girls in the primary school are closely bound up with the emancipation of women teachers. In this context there is still a lot to be done.

CONCLUSIONS

As both practical experience and research studies at intracultural and intercultural level show, girls in the primary school achieve better grades than boys. At the same time, they are confronted with many problems concerning curriculum content and social and personal interrelations with their male schoolfellows and their teachers (both female and male).

School, the first and most important social and cultural environment outside the family, shows little commitment to the needs and interests of girls. Consequently, in the primary school the girl begins to take her first steps on the long one-way road of discrimination. This will continue as a result of different factors affecting her personal development and her professional career. She will receive continual reinforcement of the predetermined (sexual) nature of her position in society.

Even though various groups at different levels in NRW have pushed for greater sex equity and equal opportunities in the primary school, the results are rather limited. From a pragmatic point of view, much educational campaign work has to be done among primary school teachers to bring about changes in awareness of the issues. Such campaigns have, however, to cope with the tensions between the cultural models which prevail in society, and the educational ethos existing in the microcosmos of the primary school.

BIBLIOGRAPHY

Brehmer, I. (ed.) (1982) – Sexismus in der Schule, Weinheim.

Der Kultusminister des Landes Nordrhein-Westfalen (1973) Richtlinien und Lehrpläne für die Grundschule in Nordrhein-Westfalen, Düsseldorf, Schriftenreihe des Kultusministers, 42.

Der Kultusminister des Landes Nordrhein-Westfalen (1985) Richtlinien und Lehrpläne für die Grundschule in Nordrhein-Westfalen, Düsseldorf, Schriftenreihe Hefte 2001–2007, Düsseldorf/Köln.

Der Kultusminister des Landes Nordrhein-Westfalen (1985) Runderlass vom 11.7.1985, I A 2, 32–40/3–429/85.

Kaiser, A. (1985) – 'Mädchen und Jungen – eine Frage des Sachunterrichts?' in: Valtin, R. und Warm, U. (eds.) – Frauen machen Schule; Probleme von Mädchen und Lehrerinnen in der Grundschule pp. 52–65, Frankfurt.

Schümer, G. 'Geschlechtsunterschiede im Schulerfolg', in: Valtin, R., Warm, U. (eds.), Frauen machen Schule; Probleme von Mädchen und Lehrerinnen in der Grundschule, pp. 95–100; Frankfurt.

Diverse articles in the pedagogic journals:
Die Grundschule (The Primary School)
betrifft: erziehung (re: education)
päd. extra (ped. extra)
Frauen und Schule (Women and School)

Conclusion

> But I still insist, that not only the virtue, but the *knowledge* of the two sexes should be the same in nature, if not degree, and that women, considered not only as moral, but rational creatures, ought to endeavour to acquire human virtues (or perfections) by the *same* means as men, instead of being educated like a fanciful kind of *half* being – one of Rousseau's wild chimeras. (Mary Wollstonecraft, *A Vindication of the Rights of Women*, 1793, reprinted in Rossi, A. (ed.), *The Feminist Papers*, Bantam, 1973, p. 54)

Mary Wollstonecraft made this plea for a proper education for girls and women almost two centuries ago, yet one can still hear claims that women are *naturally* more virtuous (or rule-following) and less rational (or scientific) than men and should be educated accordingly. How do we, the contributors to this volume and all involved intimately in the schooling systems of our respective countries, see the way forward in challenging these views?

As I mentioned in the introduction, most of the authors emphasize the importance of changing practices within the classroom, reducing the dominance of boys over girls in everyday school life, making the curriculum, particularly science and technology, more 'girl-friendly' and reviewing school staffing patterns. Some argue for a greater understanding of the processes of patriarchal values and structures as a means to implement change. The key issue, it seems, is how to make governments, teachers, parents and society as a whole, as well as pupils, aware of the necessity for providing a *proper* education for girls. Only then will sufficient resources be put into schooling to make it work in the interests of girls and women, as well as boys and men.

Once that commitment has been gained, particularly from the centre (i.e. from policy-makers at government or federal levels), the way is open for:

112

1. support for research on gender relations in education and the educational needs of women as workers, citizens and parents;
2. sponsorship of developmental projects and experimental strategies which focus on *how* to change the relationship between the sexes in schooling and in society as a whole;
3. development of guidelines on equal opportunities for teachers and other educational personnel, e.g. on staffing patterns or 'whole-school' policy;
4. production and distribution of non-sexist curricular resources and classroom materials;
5. compulsory pre- and in-service training for teachers and others involved in schooling.

However, it is also evident, particularly from the case studies, that many of those advocating greater equality in education have little support from central government. They have, thus, to rely on their own energy and commitment to make progress. However, they can, for example:

1. monitor and change their own classroom practices;
2. try to convince their colleagues and the parents of their pupils of the need for change, i.e. by working towards the development of a school equal opportunities policy;
3. work together with others concerned about inequalities in the schooling system, e.g. the teacher unions, 'women in education' groups, sympathetic parents;
4. develop strategies for gaining wider support for equality issues. For example, arguments about the growing need for more female scientists and technologists in the 1990s, when there will be a shortage of skilled labour in these areas, are likely to be of interest to employers and politicians. Focusing on the low pay and poor working conditions of the large majority of working women will find more sympathy with the parents of female pupils, possibly the girls themselves and the trade unions.

The chapters in this book, then, show very clearly how educational policy on equal opportunities has developed in different countries, according to the social, cultural, economic and political conditions that prevail. In many of the 'case-study' countries, government initiatives have led to some discussion of the issues, and voluntary groups have formed to hasten progress, yet there are still few noticeable changes at the level of the classroom. The United Kingdom is rather more advanced in terms of the development of strategies to promote equality and in analysis of egalitarianism and feminism, yet lacks firm commitment from central government. The Nordic countries have also developed sophisticated analyses, produced exciting materials and have supportive governments.

Most advanced of the countries represented in this volume, in terms of the *practical* applications of equality of opportunity, is the province of Ontario in Canada. Here, those advocating change have received support and political commitment from central government, access to sufficient funds to produce revised materials for most schools in the province, and enough 'grassroots' teacher support to make genuine changes in attitude and practice at classroom level possible.

Clearly, the strategies available to teachers across Europe will be different, based on current national economic, social and educational priorities. Furthermore, the guidelines provided on equal opportunities by, for example, the Ontario government or the British Equal Opportunities Commission, indicate the complex nature of equal opportunities work. It demands fundamental changes at attitudinal, economic and social levels. As most of the authors in this book indicate, education alone cannot be held responsible for society's evils, neither can educational reforms alone alter entrenched social attitudes and economic patterns.

However, education *can* be an important instrument for change and individual teachers have enormous influence, for good or ill, on their pupils. We must therefore look for support for greater equality in education from central government (the policy-makers) *and* the local school (the practitioners). In my view, however, the energy and commitment of the teachers themselves are the only sure guarantees that genuine educational equality can ever be achieved.

Index